FAMOUS CRICKETERS OF ESSEX

by

Dean P. Hayes

Foreword by Doug Insole

SPELLMOUNT LTD
TUNBRIDGE WELLS, KENT

In the Spellmount/Nutshell Cricket list:
The Test Match Career of Geoffrey Boycott
by C D Clark
The Test Match Career of Sir Jack Hobbs
by Clive W Porter
Cricket Anthology
by Samuel J Looker
Cricket at Hastings
by Gerald Brodribb
The Test Match Career of Walter Hammond
by Derek Lodge
Kent Cricketing Greats
by Dean Hayes
The Test Match Career of Ted Dexter
by Derek Lodge
Gloucestershire Cricketing Greats
by Dean Hayes
The Lord's Test
by Steven Lynch

First published in the UK in 1991 by
SPELLMOUNT LTD
12 Dene Way, Speldhurst
Tunbridge Wells, Kent TN3 ONX

© Dean Hayes 1991

British Library Cataloguing in Publication Data
Hayes, Dean 1949–
    Famous cricketers of Essex – (Famous county cricketers).
    1. Essex (England). Cricket
    I. Title II. Series
    796.3580922

ISBN 0–946771–85–5

Typeset by Kudos Graphics, Slinfold, West Sussex
Printed in Great Britain by
The Ipswich Book Co, Ipswich, Suffolk

DEDICATION

for Ben

who thankfully shares my enthusiasm for the game.

ACKNOWLEDGEMENTS

I am greatly indebted to the following for their help in the compilation of this book:

Peter Edwards (Essex CCC Secretary/General Manager) and for the considerable help afforded to me by Mike Marshall with facts and statistics throughout, also *Douglas Insole* who has kindly written the foreword.

Further thanks to my colleague *Peter Stafford* for his assistance with research.

The illustrations were kindly provided by *Mike Marshall*.

Finally, my thanks to *Ian Morley-Clarke* for continuing to give me the opportunity to write about Famous County Cricketers.

SELECT BIBLIOGRAPHY

D Lemmon and M Marshall: Essex County Cricket Club – The Official History 1987.

Leslie Newnham: Essex County Cricket 1876–1975, Privately Published 1976.

Christopher Martin-Jenkins: The Wisden Book of County Cricket, Queen Anne Press 1981.

Trevor Bailey: Championship Cricket, Frederick Muller 1961.

Charles Bray: Essex County Cricket, Convoy Publications 1950.

Bill Frindall: England Test Cricketers 1988.

Essex County Cricket Handbooks 1980–1989.

Wisden Cricket Monthly 1977–1989.

The Cricketer 1969–1989.

Philip Bailey, Philip Thorn and Peter Wynne-Thomas: Who's Who of Cricketers.

Lillywhite: Essex County Cricket Club Handbooks.

Leslie Thompson: Cricketing in Essex.

CONTENTS

FOREWORD

ESSEX CRICKET

For those associated with and concerned for Essex cricket at almost any time in its history, life has not been easy. Interesting, soul-destroying, exciting, frustrating, exhilarating – all these things it has been, and not infrequently all on the same day – but it has not often been dull.

In the early days, the County Ground at Leyton with its walled surround and its generally placid pitch was the home of Essex cricket, but the need to take the game into non-metropolitan parts of the county was quite soon recognised and when, in the 1920s, fixtures were moved out to such far-flung outposts of Empire as Colchester, Chelmsford and Southend the Club and its players were obliged to adapt to new and changing circumstances.

For about 40 years Essex were nomads. A club without a permanent home. Several Essex grounds were among the most attractive in the country, but the variability of pitches, interesting as it was, made it difficult for the players to perform consistently, and it was only when our 'home' ground, at Chelmsford, was purchased in the late 1960s that the seeds of future success were sown.

When some tangible success did come, in 1979, it was all the sweeter for having been so long in the making, but almost as noteworthy as the eventual triumphs in the County Champion-ship and the other domestic competitions is the fact that, even without cups and trophies, Essex cricket in the first 102 years of its existence managed to maintain a reputation for quality, enterprise and personality that regularly placed our teams among the major attractions in the country.

'Characters' a-plenty there have been, many of them as unpredictable as the performances of the Essex teams in which they played. The cricketing deeds of most of them are recorded in this book, but in many instances the manner of their performances have been more interesting than their statistical significance.

Essex have, until fairly recently, not had much of a spin attack, but pace bowlers we have produced in large numbers. Charles Kortright was one of the first and probably the fastest of this particular breed, and he was followed down the years by Johnny Douglas, Hopper Read, Ken Farnes, Morris Nichols, Trevor Bailey, Barry Knight, John Lever and, latterly, Neil Foster and Derek Pringle – all of them England bowlers, and several of them all-rounders of outstanding quality.

Essex have appointed many fewer captains than any other County in the past fifty years – just seven in fact – and in so doing have given the Club a sense of stability even in troubled times, which have not been infrequent. Most notably, of course, the two latest Essex captains, Keith Fletcher and Graham Gooch, have also led the England team.

Two Essex captains, Peter Perrin and Tom Pearce, were very unlucky not to be selected for England, although both had spells as England selectors and the latter's contribution to our Club as Chairman, President and most other things as well, has been priceless. We should remember that two early Essex captains, F L Fane and J W H T Douglas, skippered England with distinction.

There are many other distinguished batsmen, bowlers and administrators, too numerous to mention, whose contributions to Essex and England cricket certainly merit recognition in this introduction, but I would like to think that the greatest attraction of Essex cricket over past years has been the manner and the spirit in which it has been played by cricketers of vastly varying capabilities who have represented our County. It is that aspect of Essex cricket which has sustained and enhanced my own interest in the Club over very many dramatic, exciting and enjoyable years and which has, I suspect, inspired the loyalty of many other Essex devotees.

D.J. Insole

INTRODUCTION

Although the Essex County Cricket Club as we know it today, was formed in 1876, it is accepted that there were earlier county teams. The earliest reference to cricket in Essex is the report of a match at Richmond on Monday 23 August 1731. The St James's Evening Post advertised this match as being between ten men of Middlesex and ten men of Essex. The Essex side was to be led by Lord Richmond, 'the Duke who was Cricket' yet as he was associated with Slindon in Sussex, it is much more likely that the contestants were actually Surrey and Sussex who had met a week earlier at Chichester.

There are references to matches played in the eighteenth and early part of the nineteenth century by Essex sides. In 1732, London met Essex and Hertfordshire in Epping Forest for £50 a side and three years later, cricket was being played on Woodford Green and Shenfield Common, where Romford beat Brentwood there by 37 'notches'. By the second half of the eighteenth century, cricket was being played all over Essex. Perhaps the most famous of these matches was the meeting at Tilbury Fort in 1776 between Essex and Kent. There was a dispute over the qualification of one of the Kent players. The game ended in a riot, resulting in the deaths of the Sergeant in charge of the Fort, a soldier and one member of the Essex side.

'Doubts about the authenticity of this account were raised by Leslie Thompson in an article in the "Essex Countryside" magazine, which was also included in his privately published book "Cricketing in Essex". Thompson queried the truth of this report on several counts, such as the date, venue and lack of further evidence or news as to whether the miscreants escaped completely or were apprehended and charged. The account appears, however, to have been accepted elsewhere but presumably cannot now be proved either way.'

However, by 1787, when the two counties met again, this time at Swanscombe, relationships still appear to have been strained. Essex won by an innings and Kent refused to drink with their conquerors! The first Lord's ground, named after Thomas Lord was the scene of the first cricket match between Essex and Middlesex on 31 May and 1 June 1787. It is believed to be the first cricket match of any importance ever to be played on any of the Lord's grounds: Middlesex beat Essex by 93 runs.

The first mention of an Essex County Club is to be found in 1790. A year later, Essex met MCC in a three-day match at Hornchurch, but were beaten by 116 runs. In 1793, the result was reversed when Essex won at Lord's by three wickets.

By 1808, the strong Homerton club were beaten twice by Essex at Lord's and Woodford Wells, both sides having several 'given men'. It is believed that the Essex captain on this occasion was Lord Frederick Beauclerk, but it is not easy to discover who actually captained the sides.

The 'county' organisation seems to have lapsed over the next few years, but by 1816, the Sporting Magazine reports 'Several well contested matches of cricket were played this month in Essex. The game was played with the new regulation stumps 26 inches, popping crease 4 feet, which seems to be generally adopted. Bats as usual, and laws as before.' By the following year, the resurgence of Essex cricket seemed complete, when the Chelmsford Chronicle wrote: 'We are glad to see the spirit of this noble game reviving in this county'.

By the middle of the nineteenth century, the emphasis of Essex cricket had moved from South to North. The great days of Hornchurch were at an end, the strength of Essex cricket being found primarily on Lord Braybrooke's estate at Audley End, where several matches of importance were played.

A County Cricket Club was established at Chelmsford around 1859–60. It doesn't appear to have lasted long and couldn't match the full sides of other counties such as Cambridgeshire, Norfolk and Surrey and against strong club sides as Southgate. However, twice in the next decade, Essex showed they were a match for the very best. On 1 and 2 July 1861, Essex beat Surrey in a thirteen-a-side match at the Kennington Oval by 158 runs and followed this five years later by defeating MCC by one wicket. The number of first-class counties was now ten, but Essex still had no county club. Then on 7 January 1876, the following notice appeared in the Chelmsford Chronicle:

A Public Meeting will be held at the Shire Hall, Chelmsford on Friday 14th January, 1876, at three o'clock, to consider the desirability of forming a county cricket club with a ground at Brentwood.

Signed:
I E Perry Wallington
James Round

The chair at this meeting was taken by James Round, Member of Parliament for Colchester. He devoted a great deal of his time to assisting the club in its formative years and was both Chairman and Captain of the club until 1882.

James Round was born in Colchester on 6 April 1842 and educated at Eton, for whom he played against Harrow at Lord's in

1860. He went up to Christ Church, Oxford, captaining the College XI and developing into one of the best amateur wicket-keepers of the day. He was chosen for the Gentlemen in their fixture against the Players, but surprisingly did not receive his Blue.

On 13 and 14 June 1876, Essex participated in what is generally regarded to be their first county match, when they defeated Suffolk at Ipswich by eight wickets. Charles Edward Green captained the side from 1883 until 1888. He was born at Walthamstow on 26 August 1846 and educated at Uppingham and later Cambridge. Initially a fast opening bowler, he turned his attention to his batting, turning in many heroic performances. Green was a man who could turn his hand to any sport. At the Walthamstow Rifle Club Sports in 1866, he had won six events – kicking the football, 100 yards, high jump, long jump, hurdles and throwing the cricket ball! In 1884, he and F H Stevens added 129 for the sixth wicket against Northamptonshire at Wellingborough in what was the first large stand for the new county club. Green should not just be remembered for his performances on the field for he took the club into a new age. He persuaded F H Stephenson to become cricket coach at Uppingham and it was from his connection with Uppingham that he was able to persuade A P Lucas to come to Essex. Green brought a new spirit and a sense of ambition to the side.

The early sides were predominantly amateur but Essex had two notable exceptions in Henry Pickett and Frank Silcock. Pickett was strongly built and bowled quickly: he served Essex well for 16 years. He took 10 for 32 against Leicestershire at Leyton in 1895 and yet finished on the losing side. He is one of only two Essex players to have taken all ten wickets in an innings.

During the years 1876 to 1893, Essex was listed in cricket reference books under the heading of 'Minor Counties' and then later under 'Other Counties'. By the year 1885, it had become evident that the club could not hope to continue with the poor level of support at Brentwood. A decision was taken to purchase a ground in east London, a more populated area. This led the County into purchasing the Lyttelton ground at Leyton in 1886 for £12,000. This was to be the County's headquarters for almost fifty years.

In the first full Leyton season, Essex played Derbyshire, Hertfordshire, Lancashire, Norfolk and Surrey in home and away matches with additional matches at home against Staffordshire and MCC. Among other visitors to Leyton that year, were the Parsees, the first Indian team to tour this country.

By 1889, the fixture list had been reduced and the county could only claim two successes, over Leicestershire and Surrey, both at Leyton. H G Owen carried his bat for 153 and Henry Pickett took 7 for 15 as Leicestershire were dismissed for 51 in their second innings to give Essex an easy win. The more notable victory was against Surrey by 135 runs, Pickett producing match figures of 12 for 78.

The 1892 season began with the tragic suicide in early May of C D Buxton the Essex captain. He was succeeded by A P Lucas who led the county until 1894. A good season in 1893 enabled the county to gain first-class status the following season. They beat Derbyshire, Hampshire, Leicestershire, Surrey and Yorkshire at Sheffield. H G Owen became Essex captain in 1895, the County's first season in the County Championship, when they won five Championship matches. In beating Somerset that summer, they scored 692 which was only beaten in May 1990 when they scored 761 for 6 against Leicestershire at Chelmsford. Essex enjoyed a very successful season in 1897, challenging strongly for the County Championship title right up to the end of the season. Even Wisden commented 'the most striking feature of the 1897 season was the rise of Essex . . .'. Essex were indeed a striking force. They beat Yorkshire twice and Lancashire the champions once, being very unlucky to lose the battle at Old Trafford. They eventually finished third, a position they didn't better until 1978! Without doubt, the highlight of the 1899 season was a fine win over the touring Australians by 126 runs.

As a 'new' county, Essex had many headline makers in the years leading up to the outbreak of World War One. The county possessed two players, Charles Kortright and Percy Perrin: two of the best never to play for England.

Charles Kortright remains one of the fastest bowlers of all-time. He bowled as fast and as straight as he could, with no thought about swing and cut. It is hightly probable that many of his victims were frightened and of the 297 wickets he took between 1895 and 1898, 201 were clean bowled! Derbyshire batsman, G Walker, described his first meeting with Charles Kortright: 'The first ball was coming back over my head from the wicket-keeper when I got my bat down; the second was in the keeper's hands when I made my stroke and the third knocked one of my stumps back to the wicket-keeper before I knew what to do'. Kortright was very fast indeed: Sir Pelham Warner placed him with Harold Larwood as the fastest bowler he ever saw.

Percy Perrin was a superb player of fast bowling; he hit 65 centuries for Essex and made 29,172 runs. He took centre stage in one of county cricket's most remarkable games. At Chesterfield in 1904, Essex scored 597 in their first innings, Perrin making 343 not out. Derbyshire replied with 548 and then dismissed Essex for 97. Derbyshire with Ollivierre scoring 92 not out (following his 229 in the first innings) knocked off the required runs to win by nine wickets, inside three days. His lack of agility in the field was said to be the reason for his not being chosen for England. He eventually became chairman of selectors, and his judgement was held in high regard.

Other notable Essex batsmen of this time were: Charlie McGahey who was a consistent run-scorer for twenty seasons; he was a 'character' who was at one time, assistant secretary and ended up as scorer; Frederick Fane, a most attractive stroke-maker and 'Bob' Carpenter who was especially strong on the back foot.

On the bowling front, Walter Mead was the first Essex man to take 100 wickets in a season. He could bowl both off and leg spin and twice took 17 wickets in a match. He was known as the 'Essex Treasure' and took 1,916 wickets in a career spanning from 1894 to 1913. 'Sailor' Young was a gifted left-arm bowler, well supported by F G Bull and Claude Buckenham.

William Reeves was a good all-rounder, a free, hard-hitting batsman and right arm medium-pace bowler, but the most gifted and determined of the Essex all-rounders was Johnny Douglas who first played for Essex in 1901 and became captain some ten years later. His staunch batting and swing bowling made him a household name in both England and Australia.

For some years though, the Club's financial position had been somewhat precarious and things came to a head in the winter of 1907–08. The crisis was avoided when Johnny Douglas' father took up one of the Club's mortgages on the Leyton ground for £5,000. In 1912, the club were rocked by another financial upset: Charles Green, the club chairman resigned. This was a great blow, as Mr Green had helped the County financially on many occasions.

The last season before the First World War, 1914, was a successful one, with the Club winning nine of its matches.

There were perhaps more downs than ups in the early years after World War I. Some players had retired and others were coming to the end of their careers. However, the excellence of the square at Leyton, usually assured the County of plenty of runs at home. The ever-present financial problems caused the Club to try and sell the ground to the Army Sports Control Board in 1922, thereby wiping out all the mortgages that had been crippling the Club for years. A condition of the sale was that the Army granted the county the right to use the ground for most of its home matches.

Johnny Douglas as captain was certainly leading by example, as two magnificent performances in consecutive matches go to show; he hit 123 not out and took 14 for 156 against Worcestershire and then scored 210 not out and took 11 for 47 against Derbyshire.

Percy Perrin was going strong, but new and promising players such as Cutmore, Freeman, Nichols, O'Connor and Russell were coming to the fore. Essex also had two other players in Hubert Ashton and Leonard Crawley, both brilliant players. Ashton had to put business before cricket from 1921 onwards and Crawley, who hit a magnificent 176 not out to give Essex victory over Sussex against the clock in 1927, could also only play irregularly. In 1924, the Essex club faced yet another financial crisis, necessitating a public appeal for £1,000. At a Special Meeting, the Committee was reconstructed on a basis of direct representation of various districts with a view to increasing the interest in cricket throughout the county.

A B Hipkin, a discovery of Johnny Douglas was a slow left-arm spinner who in 1924 took 109 wickets at a cost of 20.34. He could on a 'sticky' pitch be more or less unplayable. At Blackpool that season, he did the 'hat-trick' against Lancashire, a side renowned for its batting. 'Jack' Russell was by now fully established as an opening batsman of the highest calibre. In 1920, he had become the first Essex batsman to score 2,000 runs in a season and in 1923, scored 140 and 111 in the fifth Test at Durban, the first time an Englishman scored two separate hundreds in a Test match. He went on to make 71 hundreds in an outstanding career.

In 1925, Johnny Douglas developed appendicitis, necessitating an operation during the winter. He was regarded by Jack Hobbs as the best opening bowler he ever encountered. Douglas was a dour, uninteresting yet courageous batsman, who scored 17,915 runs and took 1,443 wickets for Essex in a career that ended in 1928 when, after a disastrous season, the Committee asked him to resign. He refused and H M Morris was appointed in his place. It was tragic that the career of such an outstanding player as Johnny Douglas should end this way. In 1930, Douglas was drowned, together with his father when the steamer in which they were sailing was in a collision in thick fog in the Kattegat. Douglas could evidently have saved himself, but went down below to save his father and neither of them were seen again.

The real problem with the Essex sides in the years immediately after the war was the bowling. Douglas fought a willing, but often hopeless battle against the odds, supported by George Louden, a fast bowler who had joined Essex from Ilford.

Jack O'Connor, another batsman good enough to play for England, made his Essex debut in 1921; he was to become a prolific run scorer for the county. His record of nine centuries in a season, which he achieved in 1929 and 1934 is held jointly with Doug Insole. His run aggregate of 2,308 in that year was a record for fifty years, standing until 1984, when Graham Gooch overtook it.

Lawrie Eastman was a sparkling all-rounder for Essex in this period, but perhaps it was Stan Nichols who did most for Essex in the years leading up to the outbreak of World War Two. Nichols was a solid left-handed batsman and a superb right-arm fast-medium bowler. In 1929, he became the first Essex professional to perform 'the double' with 1,301 runs and 104 wickets. In fact, he was to do 'the double' eight times between 1929 and 1939. He could be fairly counted amongst the most formidable all-round cricketers. From 1924 to 1939, he scored 15,736 runs and took 1,608 wickets.

In 1933, Tom Pearce and Denys Wilcox were appointed joint captains, during which season the county finished fourth with 13 wins. At the end of that season, it was decided to leave Leyton, and Chelmsford became the County headquarters. Weeks had been held at Southend since 1906, Colchester since 1914, Chelmsford since 1925 and Clacton since 1931. To these were added Brentwood and Westcliff, with Ilford being included in the following year.

In 1935, the County beat the South Africans by 7 wickets and at their best were capable of beating anyone, as they showed when they met Yorkshire at Huddersfield. After three years of being on the receiving end of Yorkshire's record opening stand of 555, they bowled them out for just 31 runs (at one stage they were 9 for 6) and 99. Stan Nichols had a superb match, taking 11 for 54 and making 146 out of Essex's total of 334. The story is told of the Yorkshire Committee man who arrived a little late on the first day and asked the gate-man for the score. 'Thirty for nine' came the reply. 'Thirty for nine, eh,' replied the committee man. 'Champion, champion. How many wickets has Bowes got?' 'Bowes?' came the gate man's retort. 'Bloody Bowes is batting!'

On the bowling front, Nichols was joined by 'Hopper' Read, who took 9 for 62 in that famous victory over the white-rose county. He was a really fierce fast bowler who sacrificed accuracy for speed, but was a match-winner on his day. The formidable six foot five inches, broad shouldered Kenneth Farnes was a very fast bowler indeed at times and, in the last season of cricket before the hostilities, had taken 16 wickets in a match at Clacton, including a hat-trick. He had been chosen as one of Wisden's 'Five Cricketers of the Year' but wasn't to return in 1946, as he Eastman and Claude Ashton were casualties of the war.

Also in support were Ray Smith, a fast-medium bowler and his cousin, Peter, a spinner and more than useful batsman.

During the three years prior to the Second World War, Essex played consistent cricket, finishing 6th, 6th and 4th in the County Championship. In the period between the war years, Essex generally had a side full of character and were on the day capable of beating anyone.

When first-class cricket resumed in 1946, Essex were without O'Connor and Nichols, who had both retired.

Tom Pearce had been appointed captain, but it was the Smith cousins who were to take centre stage over the next couple of seasons. In 1947, Peter Smith achieved 'the double' with 1,065 runs and 172 wickets. His total of 172 wickets was more than any other Essex player in history. Batting at number 11 against Derbyshire at Chesterfield, he scored 163 – a world record for the last man. He and Frank Vigar put on 218 for the tenth wicket, an Essex record, and only 31 runs short of the record in this country. Not surprisingly, he was chosen as one of Wisden's 'Five Cricketers of the Year'. In 1948, Ray Smith scored the fastest hundred of the season – Derbyshire again being the county to suffer as he hit his 100 in 63 minutes in the match at Colchester. This was also the season that Essex suffered defeat at the hands of the Australians by an innings and 451 runs at Southend. Bradman made 187 as the Aussies scored 721 in one day. Essex however, were the only county side to bowl out the Australians inside a day.

Two outstanding players came to the fore at about this time, both products of Cambridge University – Trevor Bailey and Doug Insole. It was Insole who took over the captaincy of the county from Tom Pearce in 1951. Essex, under Doug Insole's leadership, played very attractive cricket in the fifties, twice winning the trophy for the fastest scoring rate and establishing a reputation in the first-class game as a top-rate fielding side.

Doug Insole was a very effective batsman – he scored 48 centuries for Essex and was good enough to compete for an England middle-order place with the likes of Barrington and Graveney in the fifties. Insole was fully committed to the cause of county cricket as a whole and Essex cricket in particular. In 1951 he became the first Essex amateur to reach 2,000 runs in a season. Four years later, he scored 2,427 runs, reaching both 1,000 and 2,000 runs before any other batsman and scoring more runs than anyone else.

Trevor Bailey was, throughout the fifties, England's best all-round cricketer. He was a tremendous competitor in any game, who loved batting, bowling and fielding and did all three with both great determination and skill. In 1959, he scored 2,011 runs and took 100 wickets. This was the only time an Essex player achieved this particular 'double'. In 1961, he took over the captaincy from Insole, always leading by example. He was capable in the years up to his retirement in 1967 of winning a match by inspired bowling or saving it with a stubborn display of batting. In 1962, he led the Essex side to victory over Pakistan, thus becoming the first County to defeat all the major touring countries.

Other players of note for the county in this period include Paul Gibb, formerly of Yorkshire and England. He kept wicket and scored valuable runs for the county. 'Sonny' Avery was a gifted, natural batsman who in 1952 had helped Gibb set then a new county second wicket record of 294 in the match at Northampton.

Dickie Dodds was a handsome, attacking opening batsman who often gave Essex a flying start to their innings.

On the bowling front, Ken Preston was a bowler of genuine pace until an injury forced him to slow down. Barry Knight was an all-rounder of genuine class, who as a bowler became almost as effective as Bailey himself. Also during this period, the county were aided by the spin of Bill Greensmith and the brilliant fielding of Michael Bear. Thanks to financial help from the Warwickshire Supporters' association, the County was able in 1966, to purchase the Chelmsford ground. It was in this year that Essex became the first County to stage County Championship cricket on a Sunday, against Somerset at Ilford. It proved a financial success, as some 6,000 spectators attended the match. The 1967 season was a watershed in the history of the Essex County Cricket Club. The team were next to the bottom of the Championship and the club's finances were in a serious state. From 1967, Brian 'Tonker' Taylor skippered a squad of just 13 players. He was an East Londoner of great character and a firm believer in principles and discipline. The club's fortunes may have been at a low ebb, but Taylor, a wicket-keeper and batsman introduced a new spirit amongst his young players.

Taylor's right-hand-man at first was Gordon Barker, a brave and inventive opening batsman. He had other players around him who were to shape the fortunes of Essex cricket in the years to come: Keith Fletcher, a batsman of rare skill; John Lever, a fast-medium left-arm over the wicket bowler who was to establish a regular place on the departure of Barry Knight to Leicestershire; Ray East and David Acfield, a pair of very reliable off-spinners; Stuart Turner, a marvellously talented all-rounder and Keith Boyce, a Barbadian all-rounder, whose big hitting and fast bowling thrilled crowds all round the country. There was also the busy all-rounder Brian Edmeades and the highly entertaining Robin Hobbs to bolster the side.

Not surprisingly with players of this calibre, Essex became particularly adept at the newly-introduced 40 over John Player Sunday League. They finished third in 1969, fourth in 1970, second in 1971 (when they missed the title by three-thousandths of a run!) and third in 1972.

At the end of 1973, Brian Taylor retired and Keith Fletcher assumed the captaincy for the following season, soon establishing himself as a fine tactician, leading a skilful and entertaining team. The County had by now achieved financial stability and had become a power to be reckoned with in the cricketing world.

In 1976, the county finished second once again in the John Player League, losing the title on a slower scoring rate. They were runners-up again the following year, this time losing out on the number of away wins. In 1978, the Essex side experienced even more frustration when they just failed to beat Somerset in the semi-final of the Gillette Cup (the scores being level, but Somerset had lost fewer wickets) and in the County Championship, in which they finished second (higher than ever before) – the near misses were becoming more frequent.

Essex had by now acquired the services of Ken McEwan, a beautifully polished and exciting batsman; Norbert Phillip, another West Indian all-rounder, and Brian Hardie from Stenhousemuir, who began as a largely defensive player, but flourished as a highly effective run-scorer able to adapt his game to the many different situations today's cricket demands.

By now, Chelmsford had become the County ground, where more than half the home matches were staged: Festival weeks having been reduced to three, namely, Ilford, Southend and Colchester.

Then in 1979, everything came good. Under the inspired leadership of Keith Fletcher, Essex won the Benson and Hedges Cup and for the very first time, the County Championship. In fact, the Championship was won very early, after a superb start to the season. The hero was John Lever who took 99 Championship wickets and five or more wickets eight times. The hero of the Benson and Hedges Cup win was Graham Gooch, who hit a superb 120. It was the first time a century had been scored in a Benson and Hedges final. It wasn't that Essex won something at last in 1979, it was the way they did it. They enjoyed their cricket so much, seemingly laughing their way to the top.

The chief comedian was Ray East, a clever slow left-arm bowler, who once took a hat-trick in a Test trial. In 1979, he was twelfth man against the Indians and when he brought out the drinks, the Essex players formed an orderly line to receive their refreshments. East walked straight past them and on to Yashpal Sharma, the Indian batsman who didn't want a drink. He put the drinks tray on the turf, sat down besides Sharma and started chatting. Rather sheepishly, the Essex players made their way one by one to get their drinks.

In 1980, Essex suffered a slight reaction to the heady year of 1979. They still reached the final of the Benson and Hedges Cup, losing to Northamptonshire and tied with Surrey in the Gillette Cup semi-final, losing out because Surrey had lost fewer wickets.

Around this time, a young up and coming right-arm fast bowler was making his mark in the Essex 1st XI, his name was Neil Foster.

In 1981, Essex won the John Player League title for the first time, repeating the feat three years later. In 1983, they won the county championship by 16 points and reached the final of the Benson and Hedges Cup, losing by four runs to Middlesex. This year also saw them bowl out Surrey for 14 in a County Championship match at Chelmsford. This was the lowest total against the county and was only two runs more than the all-time record low of 12. Norbert Phillip took 6 for 4 and Neil Foster 4 for 10.

In 1984, the County won the Championship title after a close finish with Nottinghamshire and also won the John Player Special League Trophy by a clear eight points. The following year, Essex beat Nottinghamshire by one run in the Nat West Trophy final. Graham Gooch (91) and Brian Hardie (110) put on 202 for the first wicket – the highest partnership in any Lord's Final. The county also reached the final of the Benson and Hedges Cup, losing to Leicestershire. This was also Keith Fletcher's last season as captain. He handed over to Graham Gooch, becoming his deputy and playing when he felt like it. The County's debt to Keith Fletcher is immeasurable – he had led the county through the greatest period of glory in Essex cricket history. For the 1986 season, the county signed Australian captain Allan Border to replace Ken McEwan. He played for the County for most of the season, scoring 1,385 runs at an average of 49.46, including four centuries. The side won the County Championship for the third time in four years and the fourth time in eight years – a successful start to Graham Gooch's reign as captain.

Graham Gooch has, since making a 'pair' on his Test debut at Edgbaston in 1975, established himself as an International player of really outstanding ability. The experience that Graham gained as captain whilst Keith Fletcher was in the side, has been a great bonus to both Essex and England, whom he now skippers. The County came close to winning the County Championship in 1988, 1989 and 1990, finishing third in 1988 and second the following two years. Also in 1989, the Essex side reached the Benson and Hedges Cup Final, losing off the last ball to Nottinghamshire. They gained their revenge in the Refuge Assurance Cup, beating the same Nottinghamshire side by 5 runs.

Last season the county scored their highest first-class total, 761 for 6 declared against Leicestershire, with Paul Prichard scoring 245 and Graham Gooch 215.

The last decade or so in Essex cricket has been a marvellously successful period. Many have been involved in the county's cause, both working hard and showing great enthusiasm.

At the time of writing, ten titles have been won and many almost achieved as the County lost off the last ball.

For the record:

County Championship:	1979	1983	1984	1986
Benson and Hedges Cup:	1979			
John Player League:	1981	1984	1985	
Nat West Trophy:	1985			
Refuge Assurance Cup:	1989			

I don't think it will end here. For with Graham Gooch to lead them, and promising players like Nasser Hussain, Nadeem Shahid, John Stephenson and Paul Prichard, the future too seems rosy.

Since Essex became a first-class county, they have produced several fine sides and considerably more outstanding cricketers than the majority of the county clubs. This book I hope, captures the flavour of those players.

DAVID ACFIELD

Born: 24 July 1947, Chelmsford
Played: 1966–1986

FIRST-CLASS ESSEX RECORDS

Matches	Innings	NO	Runs	HS	Avge	100s
378	353	191	1,259	38	7.77	–

Runs	Wkts	Avge	BB	5wI	10wm	Ct
23,509	855	27.49	8/55	30	4	120

TEST MATCHES – 0

In 1966, the Essex spin attack was strengthened by David Acfield, a Cambridge undergraduate from Brentwood School who had narrowly missed his Blue as a Freshman. However, he was destined to gain his Blue at Cambridge and did so in 1967 and 1968 after making both his Cambridge and Essex debuts in 1966. While at Cambridge he took 6 for 69 against his County in Essex's first innings. Acfield was impressing all with his off-spin when he represented Essex after the end of term at Cambridge.

He also gained recognition at international level for England as a fencer, appearing in the Olympic Games and winning a gold medal at the Commonwealth Games in Edinburgh: additionally he was the British Sabre Champion.

During the cricket season, Acfield was growing with confidence and was one of five players capped in 1970. It was during this season that he took 5 for 14 against Northamptonshire in a John Player League match.

In the match against Glamorgan at Swansea in 1974, Acfield had assisted East and Hobbs in dismissing the Welsh side for 188. Essex were 202 for 9 when Acfield joined Stuart Turner. He was in a defiant mood, staying with Turner for over two hours, in which time, they added 122 runs for the last wicket, Acfield's share being 31. Also this season, Acfield represented the MCC against the Champion County, Hampshire, at Lord's.

When Robin Hobbs left for Glamorgan in 1975, it allowed David Acfield more chances. He responded with consistent, effective bowling performances. He took 4 for 96 and 7 for 57 against Surrey at the Oval in 1976, the season he represented the MCC again, this time against the West Indies.

In 1979, when Lancashire visited Ilford, Acfield took 4 for 11 in their second innings as the red-rose county followed on, Essex winning by an innings. Against Gloucestershire this season at Colchester, Acfield took 6 for 56 in their second innings in a game that Essex won by four wickets.

In 1981, he had his most successful season. He headed the county bowling averages with 76 wickets at 22.61 runs apiece. Against Kent at the St Lawrence Ground in Canterbury, the home side were bowled out for 166 with Acfield returning the best figures of his career, 8 for 55. As Kent chased 267 to win, they were dismissed for 126, Acfield chipping in with 3 for 58.

The County's first championship victory of 1983, brought about a remarkable bowling performance from David Acfield. Essex's opponents were Somerset, the venue Taunton. Essex totalled 262, Somerset declaring on reaching 250 (Acfield taking 4 for 106). Essex hit their runs quickly and so set the cider county to get 255 in three-and-a-half hours. After starting cautiously, Acfield took 5 for 1 in 13 balls, ended with 6 for 34 and Essex won by 141 runs.

In 1984, Acfield took 6 for 58 in a rain-affected match at Worcester, this match also saw the debut of Paul Prichard, who hit an exciting 86.

As a batsman and often at number 11, Acfield turned in quite a few performances of great resolution which were the margin between defeat and victory, though his top score for Essex is only 38 made against Nottinghamshire at Chelmsford in 1973.

If he had played in the fifties or early sixties, Acfield would have had far greater opportunity to bowl his off-spin, where as for much of his career, he has had to contend with the great predominance of seam bowlers in the Essex side.

For me, David Acfield was one of the most underrated of modern-day bowlers.

SONNY AVERY

Born: 19 December 1914, New Beckton
Played: 1935–1954

FIRST-CLASS ESSEX RECORDS

Matches	Innings	NO	Runs	HS	Avge	100s
268	453	35	14,045	224	33.60	25

Runs	Wkts	Avge	BB	5wI	10wm	Ct
627	9	69.66	1/11	–	–	119

TEST MATCHES – 0

Coming from New Beckton, Alfred Victor Avery was a natural batsman who played his early cricket in Leyton. At the age of fifteen he was an office boy in the Essex club, having a perfect view of the playing area. He had been on the ground staff a long time, showing excellent promise before being given his county debut in 1935: his perseverance being rewarded.

By 1937, he had made great advances and made 22 County Championship appearances, scoring 909 runs, including a maiden century, 109 against Nottinghamshire at Trent Bridge.

Avery was also a good footballer, playing for Leyton against Dulwich Hamlet in the 1936–37 FA Amateur Cup Final.

In 1938, Avery broke a finger, putting him out of action for six weeks. Even so, he scored 831 runs, including two centuries. One of these came at Worksop: Nottinghamshire having dismissed Essex for 58, replied with 242 to gain a lead of 184. Essex surprisingly won the game by 11 runs, Avery top scoring in both innings with 21 and 136.

The following season, he topped the Essex batting averages and helped Jack O'Connor put on 225 for the third wicket against Middlesex at Lord's.

During the war years, Sonny Avery represented the Essex and Middlesex side in opposition to Kent and Surrey. In the first of these wartime matches, he scored 96.

He carried on in 1946, where he'd left off in 1939, scoring 1,210 runs, despite missing part of the season with a broken finger. He carried his bat for 83 not out against Gloucestershire and also scored two centuries and a double hundred. His score of 210, came in the match against Surrey at the Oval, when he and Dickie Dodds put on 270 in a record-breaking opening partnership. His innings contained 20 boundaries, Avery being particulrly fearsome on anything on the leg-side.

In 1948, Avery scored 1,890 runs, including six centuries. His top score was 214 not out at Clacton, in the match against Worcestershire. It was during this match that he and Dick Horsfall put on 298, a record fourth wicket partnership. During the month of August this season, Avery scored 851 runs in 12 completed innings for an average of 70.91.

In 1949 in the match against Glamorgan at Ebbw Vale, Avery scored a century in each innings, 117 and 100.

The following season saw the county finish bottom of the championship table. In their last match against Nottinghamshire at Trent Bridge (surely Avery's favourite ground) he scored a superb 141. The match was curtailed by rain, but the club's destiny had already been decided on first innings points. He hit four centuries in 1951 and in 1952 topped the Essex batting averages, scoring 1,441 runs at an average of 41.17. It was during this season that he and Paul Gibb established a new record second wicket partnership of 294 against Northamptonshire at Northampton, Avery going on to hit 224, the hightest score of his career. He hit another double hundred the following summer, 208 not out against Glamorgan at Westcliff.

In 1954, he carried his bat through an innings for the third time, scoring an unbeaten 92 against Nottinghamshire at Trent Bridge. However, this season saw Avery suffer a loss in form. He was once again hampered by injuries and didn't appear in the second half of the season. He was now in his fortieth year and decided it was time to retire.

Sonny Avery joined the Essex staff as a left-arm spin bowler, but developed into a very good opening batsman, playing many correct yet stylish innings. He had forged many good stands with his partner Dickie Dodds, including two opening stands of over 200. He himself scored four double centuries in his 25 hundreds.

TREVOR BAILEY

Born: 3 December 1923, Westcliff
Played: 1946–1967

FIRST-CLASS ESSEX RECORDS

Matches	Innings	NO	Runs	HS	Avge	100s
482	774	152	21,460	205	34.50	22

Runs	Wkts	Avge	BB	5wI	10wm	Ct
35,042	1,593	21.99	10/90	91	10	320

TEST MATCHES – 61

Trevor Edward Bailey was a pupil at the Alleyn Court Preparatory School in Westcliff-on-Sea, of which Denys Wilcox was headmaster and like his mentor he was to proceed to both Dulwich and Cambridge. It was at Cambridge that he later joined Doug Insole, who was to become an inseparable friend.

He played his first games for Essex during the war years, impressing immediately in his opening game with 4 for 36, including three wickets in his first over! He also represented several sides at Lord's, including an England XI against a West Indian XI and the British Empire XI when on leave from the Royal Marines.

When the hostilities were over, he made his debut for Essex in 1946. Though he was only able to play in a handful of matches, he scored 412 runs and took 37 wickets. He also just missed his maiden century, scoring 97 not out in the match against Worcestershire at New Road. The following season, he scored 60 not out in the Cambridge second innings in the Varsity match with Oxford. Still only able to appear for Essex at the end of term, he took 25 championship wickets, but more important, he was able to score his maiden century, a superb 205 against Sussex at Eastbourne – it was to be his highest score in first-class cricket.

Throughout the cricketing world, Trevor Bailey is 'The Boil'. This unusual nickname originated from a visit to Switzerland in the winter of 1947–48 with the Cambridge University soccer team. The Swiss announcer was having difficulty with the longer names in the Cambridge XI and announced that 'Boiley' would play at outside right . . . and 'Boiley' it became to the remainder of his Cambridge footballing colleagues. This was subsequently abbreviated to 'The Boil' and its adoption by Freddie Brown on the Australian tour of 1950–51 ensured its permanency.

At the beginning of the 1948 season, it was decided to offer Bailey the position of assistant secretary, thus enabling him to devote his full time to playing first-class cricket after coming down from Cambridge – thankfully he accepted.

In 1949, every possible distinction came to Trevor Bailey. He was selected for the MCC in their match against New Zealand and then followed it by four successive test matches. During this four match series, he had scores of 93 and 72 not out and bowling figures of 6 for 84 and 6 for 118 (which he took in his first Test). He achieved the 'double' scoring 1,380 runs (average 35.38) and taking 130 wickets (average 24.20 each). In the match against Lancashire at Clacton that season, he took all ten wickets in the red-rose county's first innings for 90 runs. He thus became only the second Essex bowler to accomplish this feat, the other being Henry Pickett. Not surprisingly, he was chosen as one of Wisden's 'Five Cricketers of the Year'.

In 1950, he took 7 for 0 in 31 balls against Glamorgan at Brentwood. Against Glamorgan at Newport in the same year, Bailey recorded a hat-trick; his victims being J.E. Pleass, N.G. Hever and D.J. Shepherd.

At Sydney in 1950, Ray Lindwall shattered Trevor Bailey's right thumb, after he had faced the fastest attack – Keith Miller at the other end – in the world for over two hours, declining to score more than 13. Against the advice of the surgeons, he returned to do battle, and though he couldn't assert himself now, he showed great courage.

In 1951, Bailey just missed another 'double' scoring 1,096 runs and taking 91 wickets in all matches. He seemed to delight in dismissing batsmen with the first ball he bowled each season. In 1949, it had been Lancashire's Nigel Howard, this season it was Jack Robertson of Middlesex, both in fixtures against the MCC. He did well to come so close to the 'double' for he had a troublesome season with injuries; badly torn back-muscles sustained in the fourth Test depriving Essex of his services for several matches and resulting in a reduction of his pace for the remainder of the season. During the close season, he gained an FA Amateur Cup Winner's medal whilst playing for Walthamstow Avenue against Leyton.

The following season he achieved the 'double' scoring 1,513 runs at an average of 36.90 and capturing 103 wickets at a cost of 29.09 runs apiece. He achieved this with some remarkable work in the Scarborough Festival at the end of the season.

In 1953, he was appointed vice-captain, a position he was to hold until he took over as captain from Doug Insole. His appearances that summer were somewhat limited due to Test and representative appearances, but he still turned in a good all-round performance against Somerset, scoring 68 not out and taking 10 for 77 in the match. During the Test series against Australia, his innings of 71 in the fifth wicket partnership of 163 with Willie Watson saved the series for England.

In 1954, Bailey performed the 'double' scoring 1,344 runs and taking 101 wickets in all matches. He was also appointed secretary, replacing Mr H.G. Clark. In the winter tour to the West Indies, he turned in his best bowling figures in Test cricket, taking 7 for 34 at Kingston, almost winning the Test match on the first day.

The following summer, Bailey once again topped the 1,000 run mark and despite his absences whilst on Test duty, picked up 63 championship wickets at an average of 20.85 apiece.

Whilst he had the reputation for some dour performances with the bat, Neville Cardus said that he 'stonewalled with passion'. In 1955 he hit a hundred before lunch in the game against Nottinghamshire at Southend. He had a successful season in 1956, heading the Essex batting and bowling averages. He scored 1,186 runs and took 78 wickets, including three centuries, the best of which was an unbeaten 141 against Hampshire at Westcliff.

In 1957 Bailey headed the county batting and bowling averages for the second consecutive year, scoring 1,322 runs and taking 104 wickets. The West Indies that summer found him almost unplayable, Bailey taking 6 for 37 and 3 for 69 in Essex's match against the tourists at Ilford. He also took 6 for 28 against Leicestershire, though his best performance for Essex in 1957 came against Hampshire at Romford, Bailey scoring 59 and 71 not out and taking 6 for 32 and 8 for 49 to leave Essex the winners by 46 runs. In the Test match at Lord's against the West Indies, he took 7 for 44 in 21 overs. It was his 50th Test match: his victims included Walcott, Weekes and Worrell.

6

Bailey represented his country on 61 occasions, scoring 2,290 runs (average 29.74) and capturing 132 wickets at a cost of 29.21. His top score with the bat was an unbeaten 134 made against New Zealand at Christchurch in 1950–51.

Though not as successful with the bat in 1958, he took 102 championship wickets at a cost of only 16.19 runs apiece: his best performances being 8 for 29 against Derbyshire and 7 for 19 against Surrey. In 1959 Bailey scored 2,011 runs (average 46.76) with six centuries and took 100 wickets at 24.69 each. It was the first time such a feat had been performed by an Essex player. He shared in two important stands, adding 216 for the fifth wicket with Doug Insole in the match against Hampshire and 171 with Barry Knight for the seventh wicket in the game with Worcestershire at Leyton.

He had another highly successful season the following year, scoring 1,639 runs and taking 117 wickets. His all-round ability was in evidence at Headingley, as Essex defeated Yorkshire. He scored 60 not out and 46 and took 7 for 40 and 5 for 61. Against the visiting South Africans he had match figures of 9 for 100, but the county still lost.

Trevor Bailey began the 1961 season as Essex captain, a natural successor to Doug Insole, who had resigned owing to business commitments. He led by example, performing the 'double' for the seventh time, scoring 1,240 runs and capturing 133 wickets. In the match against Hampshire he had match figures of 11 for 107 as the then champion county were defeated by eight wickets.

In 1962, the 'double' was performed for the eighth time by Bailey as he scored 1,460 runs and took 125 wickets. He scored 1,568 runs the following season, but his bowling fell away, Bailey taking 79 wickets, the first time he'd failed to reach 100 for quite a few seasons. He had similar totals in 1964, scoring 1,106 runs and capturing 70 wickets. He was a little more successful in 1965, just missing what would have been his ninth 'double' scoring 1,026 runs and taking 97 wickets.

He missed the majority of the 1966 season with a leg strain and in some of the games he played he really wasn't fit enough. Trevor Bailey stepped down from the Essex captaincy at the end of the 1966 season and was granted a testimonial in 1968. He played his last game in 1967, his retirement being a quite irreparable loss to Essex cricket.

After his retirement from the first-class game, he became an important member of the BBC Radio commentary team.

Trevor Bailey was always in the game; such a cricketer cannot be measured by statistics, though his are impressive enough. The great thing about him has always been his intelligence and character. He is without doubt in my mind, the finest all-round cricketer ever to play for Essex.

GORDON BARKER

Born: 6 July 1931, Bramley, Leeds
Played: 1954–1971

FIRST-CLASS ESSEX RECORDS

Matches	Innings	NO	Runs	HS	Avge	100s
444	797	46	21,895	181*	29.15	30

Runs	Wkts	Avge	BB	5wl	10wm	Ct
200	5	40.00	2/34	–	–	232

TEST MATCHES – 0

As a youngster just out of school, Gordon Barker learnt much of his early cricket in the tough Bradford League with other players like Ray Illingworth and Doug Padgett.

In 1954, he was completing his National Service as a physical training instructor in the Royal Corps of Signals and during this period represented the Army at cricket, beating both the Navy and the RAF at Lord's. He hit a century against the Navy and 67 not out against the RAF. These two years in the forces gave him the opportunity to play in a class of cricket above that which he had previously experienced. He was discovered playing in a match at Richmond by Doug Insole and Trevor Bailey and was given a trial by Essex. He made a dismal start against the touring Canadians being dismissed for 0, but he came back strongly in the second innings with 107 not out. It was obvious that Essex had made a great discovery – a ready-made successor to Sonny Avery as opening batsman.

He was known as 'The Great Bark' and was a very attractive batsman to watch, his favourite shots being the cut and hook.

In his first full season of county championship cricket in 1955 Barker scored 1,494 runs at an average of 27.66. He was immediately awarded his county cap. He scored his runs very quickly and proved to be the ideal opening partner for Dickie Dodds.

In 1957, Barker and Dodds gave the county yet another good start, rattling up 159 before lunch in the match against Kent at Clacton. In Dickie Dodds' benefit match against Middlesex at Leyton, Essex won by 74 runs with Barker scoring 117 in Essex's second innings.

In 1958, Essex beat Nottinghamshire by an innings and 112 runs at Trent Bridge, the highlight of the game being a superb 157 by Gordon Barker. The following season, Barker scored 1,432 runs at an average of 28.07. He hit another 157, this time not out in Essex's victory by six wickets over Leicestershire at Grace Road.

Soccer too was a strong interest for several years and he played on the wing for five seasons with Southend United at Roots Hall in the third division, followed by spells with both Chelmsford and Romford, until a muscle injury compelled him to abandon the sport.

Barker had another good summer in 1960, scoring 1,741 runs in all matches at an average of 36.27, including two centuries.

In 1961, Barker settled into another successful opening partnership, this time with Geoffrey Smith, following the departure of Dickie Dodds. He scored 1,740 runs at an average of 34.11. It was during this season that Gordon Barker made his highest score, 181 not out in the 166 run victory over Kent at Colchester, including getting to his hundred before lunch.

In 1962, he had the dubious distinction of dropping a chance off Jim Laker's first ball on his debut for Essex against Derbyshire.

In 1964, the Australian tourists were defeated by six wickets at Southend, Gordon Barker hitting 123, before being bowled by Graham McKenzie. Barker was now forming a third successful opening partnership pairing with Michael Bear. A senior professional in the Essex side he did on occasions lead the club in Bailey's absence.

Barker began the 1965 season in superb form but then had to miss a few games due to illness. He returned to play some useful innings and finish the season with 1,289 runs at an average of 29.29. Though the following season was a poor one for Essex, Barker scored 1,301 runs at 26.02.

He showed too, that he could adapt to one-day cricket and hit a fine 87 not out against Nottinghamshire at Chelmsford in a John Player League Match. This summer of 1971 was also the last for Gordon Barker. He finished top of the national averages in the John Player League, scoring 449 runs at an average of 56.12. He also established a fifth wicket partnership record of 128 with Keith Boyce made against Surrey at the Oval.

Gordon Barker was the mainstay of the Essex batting line-up for many years, often at a time when the county were struggling. On his retirement from first-class cricket, he became cricket coach at Felsted producing such outstanding cricketers as Derek Pringle and John Stephenson. An exiled Yorkshiremen, Gordon Barker gave everything for Essex.

MICHAEL BEAR

Born: 23 February 1934, Brentwood
Played: 1954–1968

FIRST-CLASS ESSEX RECORDS

Matches	Innings	NO	Runs	HS	Avge	100s
322	562	44	12,564	137	24.25	9

Runs	Wkts	Avge	BB	5WL	10wm	CT
53	0	:::::	–	–	–	113

TEST MATCHES – 0

Michael Bear joined Essex in 1954, hailing from Brentwood. His batting was very correct and the majority of his strokes were textbook stuff. He made his maiden century against Gloucestershire at Romford in 1957, having come very close with 98 against Kent at Clacton the previous season. However, halfway through the 1958 season he lost his form and played in the 2nd XI: yet despite this, he had amassed 913 runs in the matches he'd played in, and was awarded his county cap.

Michael Bear soon earned a reputation as a fielder who could pick-up and throw-in all in one movement, his fame soon spreading throughout the first class scene.

In 1959, Bear scored 896 runs at an average of 22.40, but as his captain said, he saved around ten runs per innings in the field. In fact, Bear's superb work in the field was being talked about throughout the land.

Bear was switched to open the Essex innings in the absence of Geoff Smith in 1962. It worked well, Bear having his most successful season, showing much more consistency in scoring 1,612 runs at an average of 29.85, including two centuries.

In 1963, Bear had another good season, hitting 1,170 runs at an average of 30.00. He unfortunately broke his leg, causing him to miss the last six games of the summer. In 1964, Bear continued to bat well when other Essex players were struggling to find their form, He scored 1,567 runs at an average of 29.56. In the match against Gloucestershire at Bristol, Essex were chasing 181 in 150 minutes to win the game. They won by six wickets and with ten minutes to spare, Bear hitting a quick-fire unbeaten 81.

In 1965, he had rather a disappointing season, hitting 772 runs, less than half his previous season's total.

However, he was back to his best in 1966, scoring 1,833 runs at an average of 32.15. Though only scoring one century, he topped the Essex batting averages at the end of the season.

He was also a useful member of the Essex side in one-day cricket. In the Gillette Cup victory over Derbyshire at Chesterfield, Bear top scored with 71 as Essex reached 200 for 8 to win by two wickets with two overs to go.

Michael Bear scored over a thousand runs in four seasons, and his fielding throughout his first-class career was outstanding. A more than useful county cricketer, Michael Bear had to retire at the end of the 1968 season due to injury.

KEITH BOYCE

Born: 11 October 1943, St Peter, Barbados
Played: 1966–1977

FIRST-CLASS ESSEX RECORDS

Matches	Innings	NO	Runs	HS	Avge	100s
211	319	18	6,848	147*	22.75	3

Runs	Wkts	Avge	BB	5wl	10wm	Ct
15,704	662	23.72	9/61	30	6	181

TEST MATCHES – 21

As a youngster in the Caribbean, he played cricket and football wherever there was a stretch of grass, a strip of matting or a sandy beach. His life was built around school and sport, though his love of sport brought him many a cuff around his ears for being late home, but it never stopped him being late again the next day. After leaving his junior school, he attended Coleridge Parry Secondary School and it was here that he wore pads and batting gloves for the first time. He also captained the school side, bowling quick to open and then reverting to leg breaks if the wicket was turning a little. Batting came naturally to Keith Boyce and by the age of twenty he was representing Barbados in inter-island cricket.

He had been seen by Trevor Bailey during the Rothman Cavaliers tour of the West Indies in 1964–65 and had been included in the Bajaan team in their second match against the touring Cavaliers. He impressed Bailey with his all-round performance – his hitting power, fast bowling and tremendous fielding. The outcome of this was that Trevor had Keith earmarked as a future Essex player. He followed the tourists to England to commence qualifying in 1965. Most Saturdays he appeared for Walthamstow and the small crowds soon began to appreciate his all-action type of cricket.

The young all-rounder from Barbados had a wonderful debut, made whilst serving his qualifying period. The opponents were Cambridge University, Boyce taking 9 for 61 and 4 for 47.

In 1967 he made his first appearance in the County Championship. He came very close to achieving the 'double' in that first season: he made over 900 runs, took 81 wickets and was given his county cap. He provided the spark that Essex cricket needed at that time. He was a most electrifying batsman and most certainly, a very fast bowler. He was also a very capable fielder, taking 33 catches this season, six of them coming in the match against Hampshire at Bournemouth.

He hit his maiden century against Hampshire at Valentine's Park in the month of June 1969. His unbeaten 147 was made in three hours and contained 21 fours. He also hit 50 in twenty three minutes against Lancashire in a John Player League match, out of Essex's total of 265. This was also the season when his all-round ability won him a single wicket tournament at Lord's.

Boyce was an Essex man through and through, in spite of playing on a regular basis for Barbados and later in his career, representing the West Indies. The Essex crowds thrilled to Boyce's exploits – his great determination to win every game was apparent for all to see. He was a most exciting and unpredictable player. He was a great one-day cricketer, possessing the ability to change the course of a match within a couple of overs, with either bat or ball.

In the John Player Sunday League at the beginning of the 1971 season, Boyce hit a magnificent 98 off only 54 balls in 50 minutes. He hit seven sixes and 11 fours, Essex defeating Surrey at the Oval by 22 runs. He destroyed Northamptonshire at Ilford, taking 4 for 10 off his 8 overs as the midland side were dismissed for 45. He performed the hat-trick this summer against Somerset at Westcliff, also in the John Player League, his victims being Robinson, Moseley and Taylor. He also destroyed Lancashire in the Sunday competition on a wet day (what else?) at Old Trafford with figures of 8 for 26.

He enjoyed a magnificent season in 1972, almost achieving the 'double'. In the Gillette Cup match against Middlesex at Chalkwell Park, Westcliff, they bowled out Middlesex for 41, Boyce taking 5 for 22 and Essex winning by eight wickets.

In 1973, he gave a superb all-round performance to lead Essex to a two-day victory over Surrey. When the West Indies beat England at the Oval by 158 runs, Boyce batting at number 9, hit 72 and then followed it with 5 for 70 and 6 for 77.

In 1974, he performed the hat-trick again; the opponents were Warwickshire with Boyces's victims Abberley, Murray and M.J.K. Smith. He was also chosen for inclusion in Wisden's 'Five Cricketers of the Year'.

In May 1975, he turned in a magnificent performance against Leicestershire at Chelmsford on a wicket that was damp and turning. Essex scored 300, Boyce hitting 113 (his hundred taking 58 minutes). By the end of the day, he had taken 5 for 25 and held two catches. His final figures in Leicestershire's first innings were 6 for 25, following it with 6 for 48, as Essex just failed to win the game. His century was the fastest hundred for 38 years and contained eight sixes and seven fours. Two weeks later, he hit a century in 70 minutes, going on to reach 123 in the Benson and Hedges Cup match against Minor Counties (South) at Goldington Bury, Bedford.

During the 1976 season, Boyce was forced to miss many matches with a knee injury. It came as a great loss when, after a serious knee operation, he was forced to retire.

He started the following season off well, taking 4 for 48 against Nottinghamshire at Ilford, but it was clear to all that he was struggling. His last match was against the touring Australians at Chelmsford where he took 4 for 90 and 1 for 19, his last wicket in first-class cricket being that of opener Rick McCosker.

He was a fast bowler who was quick enough to unsettle the greatest of batsmen and a batsman with a superb eye – his unconventional hitting changing the course of a game within a couple of minutes. He was a great hit with the Essex supporters.

Keith Boyce was a dedicated Essex cricketer. When he was given the news that he wouldn't be able to play again, he asked the Essex committee to keep his registration just in case he got better.

CLAUDE BUCKENHAM

Born: 16 January 1876, Herne Hill
Died: 23 February 1937
Played: 1899–1914

FIRST-CLASS ESSEX RECORDS

Matches	Innings	NO	Runs	HS	Avge	100s
258	394	63	4,882	124	14.74	2

Runs	Wkts	Avge	BB	5wl	10wm	Ct
24,629	934	26.36	8/33	72	16	143

TEST MATCHES – 4

Claude Percival Buckenham was born in Herne Hill, Surrey on 16 January 1876. He was educated at Alleyn's school, Dulwich but became associated with cricket at Leyton, making his Essex debut in 1899.

In 1903, he destroyed Surrey in the match at Leyton, taking 8 for 53 – it was a season when he showed great promise. The following summer, Essex won only three championship matches; the first being at Leyton at the beginning of June against Sussex when Buckenham returned what were to be his career best bowling figures, 8 for 33. He took 66 wickets this season, but was quite expensive.

In 1905, Essex beat the Australians by 19 runs, the only county side to do so. It came as a bit of a surprise, for Essex had lost six of their last seven matches. Buckenham and Tremlin took all 20 wickets between them, with Buckenham having figures of 12 for 137 – he ended the season with 90 wickets to his name, though he saw many chances in the slips off his bowling go down. In fact, his figures of 828 first-class wickets between 1905–11 would have been even more impressive but for some desperately poor Essex slip-catching.

During these seasons, Buckenham was rated as one of the deadliest pace bowlers in the country. He was a tall man, though rather sparingly built. Bowling with great speed and a good high delivery, he would have made a greater name for himself if he'd had stronger support in the field.

In 1906, Buckenham took 135 wickets in all matches at a cost of 24.13 runs each.

In 1908 he was chosen to play for the South against the North at the Oval; it was the benefit game for E.G. Hayes, the noted Surrey batsman. In the match, Buckenham turned in a memorable performance, taking 11 wickets for 161 runs. During the North's second innings, he made the ball break back so much, that six wickets, five of them bowled, fell to him for 68 runs.

In 1909, he was the most successful Essex bowler taking 97 wickets, though his total in all matches that he played was 130. His best performances were 8 for 59 against Gloucestershire at Leyton and 8 for 64 against Lancashire at Liverpool. His bowling was largely responsible for the two Essex victories that summer, taking 6 wickets in each innings at Derby and 6 for 40 against Derbyshire in the return fixture at Leyton. This was the season that he made the first of three appearances for the Gentlemen against the Players. Whilst still on the ground staff, he was in the MCC XI which beat Noble's Australians by three wickets. During the second fixture between the two sides, he took 6 for 98 as the Australians totalled 434.

He was chosen for Leveson-Gower's team to tour South Africa in 1909-10. He played in the first four Tests, taking 21 wickets at an average of 28.23, his best performance being 5 for 115 at Johannesburg.

His ability to hit a cricket ball hard brought him two first-class hundreds, his top score for Essex being 124. He often played a useful innings when runs were required.

In 1910, Essex began the season in great style, beating Cambridge at Fenner's, Buckenham taking 6 for 55. There was a 10 wicket victory over Yorkshire at Leyton, Buckenham taking 5 for 68. He took 118 wickets this summer, his best performance being 8 for 40 against Worcestershire at Leyton – the visitors who had only been set 84 to win, lost 9 wickets before reaching their target.

In 1911, Buckenham had 10 for 148 in the match against Kent at Tonbridge and went in to the match against lowly Sussex at Leyton with high hopes of a push towards the championship. He took 7 for 78, but bad fielding once again let the side down as Sussex went on to win by 6 wickets. The fortunes of Essex fluctuated greatly this season – one of the better performances coming when they beat Surrey by 182 runs, Buckenham taking 11 for 161. During this season, he was chosen for two Test trials, the third arranged for Old Trafford had to be abandoned. Buckenham performed well enough, but failed to make the tour party to Australia.

He took more than 50 wickets in 1912, though he didn't really come to terms with the wet conditions.

At the end of the 1912 season Buckenham decided to accept a position in Scotland. He had lost much of his pace, yet he was to return and play for the county again. Buckenham was assisting Forfarshire in Scotland but returned to play in the last five games of 1914. In the very last game, he took 3 for 42 in Somerset's first

15

innings and signed off with 7 for 37 in their second. He topped the Essex bowling averages that season with 26 wickets at a cost of slightly under 20 runs apiece.

After the First World War (where he served in the Royal Garrison Artillery) he became coach at Repton School. He died on 23 February 1937 at his home in Dundee, after a short illness, at the age of 61.

If those missed chances had been taken, I wonder just how many wickets Claude Buckenham would have taken?

FREDERICK BULL

Born: 2 April 1875
Died: 16 September 1910
Played: 1895–1900

FIRST-CLASS ESSEX RECORDS

Matches	Innings	NO	Runs	HS	Avge	100s
88	125	31	1,171	41*	12.45	–

Runs	Wkts	Avge	BB	5wl	10wm	Ct
7,923	365	21.70	9/93	29	5	41

TEST MATCHES – 0

Frederick George Bull was born in Essex on 2 April 1875. He made his county debut in 1895, a slow bowler who could make the ball break both ways. Bull always kept a good length and used his head well. In his first season in the game, he took only 15 wickets at a cost of more than 26 runs each. 'Incog' in Lillywhite's Cricketers' Annual and said 'In Mr F.G. Bull, Essex found a young player of considerable promise. It was not the season for slow bowlers, but on wickets which help the ball, he is sure to be of use, and with more experience ought to develop into a very useful all-round cricketer'.

Frederick bull was most certainly an off-break bowler of great promise and though his career was to be all too short, his promise was realised over the next four summers.

In 1896, Bull headed the county's bowling averages taking 70 wickets, though he would have wanted to forget his first game in the championship. He dropped Bobby Abel, the great Surrey batsman off Kortright's bowling when he'd only made 2 – he went on to hit 231!

In 1896, Bull was one of five Essex players involved in the Gentlemen v Players match at the Oval. He was without doubt, the hero of the match, taking 8 for 94 in the Players' first innings. At this time, Bull was only twenty years old and had been selected for this representative match purely on merit. In all matches he had captured 85 wickets at 16 runs each. His best performance in a county game that season was his 8 for 44 against Yorkshire at Bradford, though in a sensational win over the reigning champions Surrey at Leyton, he took 6 for 51 and 5 for 38 to give Essex the victory.

In 1897, Bull took 9 for 93 against Surrey, the game ending in a draw, when Abel hit 95 as Surrey finished on 269 for 7 chasing 362 to win. That same summer, Yorkshire, the reigning champions, were defeated by three wickets on a 'bowlers wicket' at Leyton; Frederick Bull taking 4 for 63 and 5 for 95. His bowling also brought Essex victories over both Hampshire and Derbyshire, where he had match figures of 13 for 156. When Essex met Lancashire at Leyton, a win would certainly have put Essex in contention for the championship title. Essex scored 290 in their first innings, Lancashire replying with 168. The wicket was so bad, neither county relished batting last. At that time, the law stated that the follow-on margin was 120 runs. Bull attempted to bowl wide towards the boundary to give the red-rose county the runs they needed to avoid the follow-on, but Arther Mold, the Lancashire quickie, realised what was happening and knocked down his own stumps! Bull finsihed with 7 for 63 and Lancashire following-on scored 234 with Bull taking 7 for 113 from 58.1 five-ball overs. Essex needing 130 to win, won by six wickets, Carpenter hitting 57 not out.

Also during that eventful summer of 1897, Bull was chosen for the Gentlemen against the Players at Lord's, but was rather expensive. Later in the season, he fared much better in the same fixture at Scarborough, taking eight Players' wickets at a cost of just over 24 runs each.

He could turn the ball both ways, though his stock ball was the off-break. Bull was an intelligent bowler and was so highly rated by Pelham Warner that he was chosen to tour America in the close season. In fact, Warner considered him the best slow bowler in England at the end of the 19th century. He had a very successful trip, taking 43 wickets at a cost of only 13.86 runs apiece, the greatest number taken by any member of the side.

There had been queries over Bull's bowling action. The legality of quite a few players' actions had been questioned and certainly not everyone thought Bull's action fair.

In 1898, he topped the one hundred wicket mark again, capturing 101 wickets at 21.40 runs each. He was chosen this year as one of Wisden's 'Five cricketers of the Year' who commented 'It is no flattery to say that on a lively pitch, Mr Bull can get more spin on the ball than any other English-born slow bowler now before the public'.

After taking over a hundred wickets in 1897 and 1898, Bull took only 65 (at 27.18 runs each) in 1899 – his short yet eventful first-class career was nearly at a close. Eventually in 1900 he gave way to Bill Reeves, Bull's form having been so indifferent.

At the beginning of the 1901 season, Bull resigned as assistant-secretary and moved up north to Blackburn to take up a business appointment. In 1904, he played for East Lancashire where he took 91 wickets at a cost of 12.54 runs each. He then served two years as professional with Perth and then returned to Lancashire to play for both East Lancashire and Rishton.

He was often a moody man, but it was a shock when on 16 September 1910, Frederick George Bull was found drowned at St Anne's-on-Sea, near Blackpool, his coat and trouser pockets being filled with stones. He hadn't been seen for two days. It was a very sad end for one who had served Essex so well, though only for a short period.

HERBERT CARPENTER

Born: 12 July 1869, Cambridge
Died: 12 December 1933
Played: 1894–1920

FIRST-CLASS ESSEX RECORDS

Matches	Innings	NO	Runs	HS	Avge	100s
262	466	24	13,043	199	29.50	22

Runs	Wkts	Avge	BB	5wI	10wm	Ct
2,163	46	47.02	4/57	–	–	220

TEST MATCHES – 0

Herbert Carpenter was born at Cambridge on 12 July 1869. He was the son of Robert Carpenter, one of the greatest batsmen of the United All-England and Cambridgeshire sides of the mid-19th century. In fact, young Herbert copied his father's style. He was very correct in his defence, straight and strong and excellent on the back foot, his favourite shot being the late-cut.

He made his Essex debut before the county had been granted first-class status in 1888, but made little impression. Two years later he was engaged as one of the ground bowlers at Leyton. He even topped the bowling averages with figures of six wickets for 66 runs! His eight innings brought him only 80 runs, but a little later in his career his batting had improved so much that he moved up the Essex order and became a cornerstone of their batting line-up.

As early as 1891, Carpenter was giving good accounts of himself as an opener. He hit a forceful 65 against Hampshire at Southampton, Essex winning by an innings, despite the absence of four regular first-teamers.

He was instrumental in helping the county to first-class status and in 1894, he opened the batting in Essex's first match as a first-class county against Leicestershire.

In 1895, Surrey beat Essex by an innings but not before Carpenter had scored a magnificent 145 in four-and-a-half hours. He also played two innings of marked contrast that summer. Essex's first victory in the Championship saw Carpenter crawl to 52 (without a single boundary) as wickets tumbled around him – Somerset being the opponents. In the return fixture at Taunton, Carpenter hit 153 in only 155 minutes, hitting a five and 26 fours, before being run out. He hit 976 runs for Essex (average 30.50) and 111 in his appearances for the MCC to give him an aggregate of 1,087 for the season – the first Essex batsman to score over 1,000 runs in a season.

By 1897, Herbert 'Bob' Carpenter was proving to be a batsman of the highest quality. He hit 141 at Edgbaston in the match against Warwickshire but Essex still couldn't force a victory. Later that summer, Essex entertained Lancashire at Leyton – a victory would place them among the contenders for the championship title. Chasing 130 to win, Carpenter carried his bat for 57 not out as the home side won by six wickets. He was carried shoulder-high to the professionals' dressing room, the hero of what was essentially a great team effort. A collection made for Carpenter amounted to £43 10s according to Wisden, though another report put it slightly higher.

In 1898, he hit 1,011 runs, including a superb 133 as Essex totalled 515 against Leicestershire at Grace Road. In 1900, he helped McGahey put on 235 for the third wicket against Sussex at Leyton, but the match was drawn. All told that season he hit 1,468 runs, including four centuries: two of his hundreds coming in matches against Derbyshire. 'Cricket' commented that 'Carpenter ought to be the most successful batsman; he has style and skill – but hitherto he has been very little favoured by fortune. His cricket this year has, however been excellent in every way.'

He exceeded 1,000 runs again in 1901, scoring centuries in both innings, 127 and 104 against Kent at Leyton. He was the second Essex batsman (after McGahey) to score two separate hundreds in a first-class match. He helped Perrin add 232 for the second wicket in this match.

He had been in dispute with the Committee in 1902 and didn't play at all in 1903. In 1904, against Surrey at the Oval, he and McGahey made 328 for the third wicket out of a total of 616 for 5 dec. He also made his highest score, missing his double hundred by one run. In 1905, he passed the 1,000 run mark again, helping Perrin put on an undefeated 208 in the match against Sussex at Leyton.

During the 1909 season, Carpenter had to withdraw from the first-class scene after only one match due to illness; he did return to play in five games later in the year, but not with much success.

In 1911, along with John Freeman, he had the unusual distinction of sharing in century partnerships in each innings of the match against Surrey at Leyton. In 1914, he hit the last of his 25 first-class centuries, 126 not out in the match against Worcester-shire at New Road, sharing in an unfinished stand of 237 with Russell.

After the war, he returned to play in the last two matches of the 1920 season, scoring 8 and 21 against Lancashire and 20 and 0 against Somerset. He was now in his 52nd year and had given 26 years to the county. He was without doubt one of the greatest professional batsmen never to play for England. He was a superb player for Essex, not just in terms of runs scored, but because of all the advice and coaching he gave to others.

JIM CUTMORE

Born: 28 December 1898, Walthamstow
Died: 30 November 1985
Played: 1924–1936

FIRST-CLASS ESSEX RECORDS

Matches	Innings	NO	Runs	HS	Avge	100s
342	593	36	15,937	238*	28.61	15

Runs	Wkts	Avge	BB	5wl	10wm	Ct
687	11	62.45	2/31	–	–	121

TEST MATCHES – 0

James Albert Cutmore a right-handed batsman from Walthamstow first appeared for Essex in 1924, making his debut against Surrey. He only played in five matches that season, but showed signs of developing into a confident and capable batsman.

In 1925, he made three useful scores, 20 and 37 against Middlesex and 35 against Gloucestershire, both games at Leyton. A month later, he scored 95 against Derbyshgire and was awarded his County cap. He celebrated this honour by making 134 not out against Lancashire, and went on to pass 1,000 runs for the season.

In 1927, he hit the only double century of his career, 238 not out against Gloucestershire, though overall this summer, he was less consistent.

In 1930, Cutmore was one of four batsmen to surpass 1,000 runs for the season, forming a regular and dependable opening partnership with Dudley Pope. To win the County Championship that season, Lancashire had to beat Essex in the final game at Blackpool. Essex needed 286 to win: they were dismissed for 111, Cutmore showing his fighting qualities with a superb 77 on a bad pitch, no other Essex player making double figures. The Essex side toasted the red-rose county as champions in champagne provided by the Lancashire President – Jim Cutmore rendering one of his songs!

In his early days, Cutmore had intended qualifying for Glamorgan (he would probably have been at home in the welsh valleys with his fine tenor voice) but Essex had heard of his success in Club cricket and signed him on.

In 1933, he once again topped the 1,000 run mark, hitting two centuries and twelve scores of over 70. He was to achieve this feat for eleven consecutive seasons from 1925.

In 1934 in the match against Kent at Gravesend, Cutmore hit an unbeaten 97 as Essex won by two wickets, reaching 166 for 8, after being 89 for 8 – all this on a badly worn wicket. Also that season when Leicestershire were the visitors to Chelmsford, Cutmore hit the winning run off the second ball of the last possible over to give Essex victory by two wickets, chasing a modest 84.

In 1935, Cutmore was instrumental in Essex beating the touring South Africans by seven wickets, hitting 72 and 59 not out. The visiting Indians also suffered at the hands of Jim Cutmore the following season at the end of May at Brentwood. Cutmore scored 137, as he and Peter Smith (105) put on 214 for the eighth wicket. After his superb hundred against the Indians, his form began to desert him. He played in only eight championship matches and totalled 208 runs from 14 innings with a top score of 45. He wasn't re-engaged for the 1937 season.

When on form, Jim Cutmore was a most entertaining batsman. He was an enigma – he had plenty of confidence, but it was often misplaced, his temperament not suited to the hurly-burly of first-class cricket.

DICKIE DODDS

Born: 19 May 1919, Bedford
Played: 1946–1959

FIRST-CLASS ESSEX RECORDS

Matches	Innings	NO	Runs	HS	Avge	100s
380	663	17	18,565	157	28.73	17

Runs	Wkts	Avge	BB	5wl	10wm	Ct
1,053	35	30.08	4/34	–	–	176

TEST MATCHES – 0

Thomas Carter 'Dickie' Dodds was one of the discoveries of the 1946 season, making his county debut against Sussex at Ilford. He had played for Middlesex 2nd XI before the war and in various army teams in the Aldershot area and in India where he made his first-class debut. In that first season, he played as an amateur, making a very impressive start. He scored 1,050 runs, including two hundreds. One of these came in the record-breaking partnership of 270 for the first wicket against Surrey at the Oval. His partner was Sonny Avery (who scored 210), Dodds scoring 103.

In fact, Dodds was such a hard-hitting opening batsman who enjoyed nothing more than facing a fast bowler, that it was quite likely he would hit the opening ball he faced for six! On his return to the dressing room after that innings against Surrey, captain Tom Pearce told him to go and get a decent cap, it was his way of telling Dodds he'd been awarded his County cap.

The following year, Dodds turned professional and became an established opening batsman of great promise. He hit 2,147 runs, yet scored only one century – a tribute to his consistency.

This season he was selected for the MCC against the South African tourists, scoring 80 and 25. Rather surprisingly, it was his last representative match. He was never considered for a Gentlemen v Players fixture or international honours. In 1948, he continued to impress, scoring 1,876 runs.

In 1951 one of the most exciting matches was the visit of South Africa to Ilford. South Africa declared their innings closed at 312 for 9, Essex replying with 319 for 7 dec, Dickie Dodds hitting a quickfire 138. The South Africans also declared their second innings at 286 for 5, Essex finishing on 255 for 5 just 25 runs short of their target.

In 1952, Dodds scored 1,801 runs at a very quick rate. Opening the innings with Sonny Avery, he scored his runs at more than 40 per hour throughout the season and was regarded as the fastest scoring opener in the country. He twice hit the first ball of an innings for six, and he did the following season when Essex entertained Sussex at Ilford, hitting the first ball of the Essex innings from Ian Thomson onto the pavilion roof!

In 1956, Dodds continued to show that he was no respecter of people. The Australians were the visitors to Southend, Dodds proceeding to hit both Lindwall and Miller all over the ground for a quick-fire 58, made out of the first 70 runs scored in the match.

Dodds missed the first six matches of the 1957 season because of a slipped disc, though he returned to help Gordon Barker add 161 against Kent at Clacton before lunch. Although failing to score a century, he batted with fine consistency to pass 1,000 runs. In the November of that year, he announced that he was going to devote the whole of his benefit fund, which amounted to £2,325, to Moral Rearmament, for which he was a tireless worker.

After scoring 1,000 runs a season on thirteen consecutive occasions from 1946, he lost his form completely in 1959. His last innings for the county was against Yorkshire at Colchester. He scored 20 in the early part of the evening against the pace of Freddie Trueman – a brief gem of an innings from one of the finest players of fast bowling on the county scene.

Dickie Dodds was without doubt one of the greatest cricket entertainers of that era.

JOHNNY DOUGLAS

Born: 3 September 1882, Clapton
Died: 19 December 1930
Played: 1901–1928

FIRST-CLASS ESSEX RECORDS

Matches	Innings	NO	Runs	HS	Avge	100s
459	746	108	17,915	210*	28.07	18

Runs	Wkts	Avge	BB	5wl	10wm	Ct
33,653	1,443	23.32	9/47	93	21	265

TEST MATCHES – 23

John William Henry Tyler Douglas was born in Clapton on 3 September 1882, having a passion engendered in him by his father to succed in all forms of sport. He sent Johnny to Moulton Grammar School near Spalding in Lincolnshire, and from there to Felsted. By the time he arrived at Felsted, he was an extremely capable sportsman, favouring athletics, boxing, fives, hockey and soccer. He had earned all this through hard work and was rewarded with the captaincy of the Felsted cricket XI in his last year.

He made his debut for Essex in 1901 against Yorkshire, being bowled by Hirst for 0 in both innings. Not the best of debuts for a player who was destined to become a great force in Essex cricket. In his third match, however, he made 61 not out against Derbyshire at Chesterfield.

Yorkshire were again the opponents in 1905, when Johnny

Douglas made his first great impact on the game. He took five Yorkshire wickets in eight balls, including the first ever hat-trick by an Essex player in first-class cricket; his victims were Rhodes, Haigh and Myers – he'd already dismissed Tunnicliffe and Hirst in the previous over. In future years, Yorkshire always seemed to bring the best out of Douglas, as though he was trying to make amends for that 'pair' in his first match.

In 1906, he was beginning to flourish as an all-rounder, scoring over a thousand runs and taking 93 wickets at a cost of 23.05 runs apiece. His best performance with the ball was 8 for 33 against Leicestershire at Southend as Essex won by five wickets. He also shared in the first Essex opening partnership of over 200, adding 209 with Frederick Fane in the match against Middlesex.

On 8 August 1908, he had his greatest triumph to date, when he scored his maiden century in first-class cricket, 102 in the drawn game against Sussex, after scoring 62 not out in the first innings. Also in 1907 he took 13 for 155 against Kent and 12 for 74 the following season against Gloucestershire, both matches being played at Leyton.

His long graduation in consolidating his county place was partly due to his talents as a middle-weight boxer (he won the 1905 Amateur Championship and the 1908 Olympic title) and as a footballer, gaining an England amateur cap against Bohemia.

In 1909, playing for an England XI against Australia, he scored 102, helping A.E. Knight of Leicestershire to put on 284 for the first wicket.

Despite his limited experience he became Essex Captain in 1911.

His reign as captain couldn't have begun better, for Yorkshire were the opponents and Douglas scored 47 and 55. He followed this with 60 and 34 in the match against Surrey and 80 against Middlesex – he was leading by example. He demanded better fielding and got it, a better team spirit and got that too. He made a brilliant 176 against Nottinghamshire at Trent Bridge and was chosen to represent the Gentlemen at both the Oval and Lord's. It was in this latter match that he was to triumph. Sidney Barnes was bowling superbly, but Douglas batting for over three hours for his 72, thwarted him. Douglas then produced a superb spell of fast-medium pace bowling to take 5 for 53. In the second innings, he scored 22 not out and took two further wickets. It was on the strength of this all-round performance that he was chosen to go to Australia. Warner was captain, but after playing in the opening match in Adelaide, he was taken ill and didn't play again. Douglas was appointed captain and after losing the first Test, he led England to four successive victories. He took 5 for 46 at Melbourne in the fourth Test, clean bowling Hill, Armstrong and Minett. He was a huge success, his stubborn batting earning him the nickname of 'Johnny Won't Hit Today!'

As a captain, Douglas was loyal to those under him and they gave him their loyalty and many of them their love in return. He was no great tactician as a captain, for he relied entirely on endeavour and inspiration. He often encouraged aspiring young bowlers by placing a half-crown on the top of the stumps when he was batting in the nets, the first one to dismiss him, gaining the reward. Charles Bray in his 'Essex – the County Series' wrote 'You either liked and respected John Douglas or you loathed him,' – there were no half-measures in people's responses.

In 1912, Douglas wasn't chosen for another Test until the last match of the triangular tournament against Australia at the Oval. This was despite scoring 1,411 runs and taking 81 wickets in a very disappointing season for the Essex side – in fact, he was the only Essex player to top 1,000 runs that summer.

In 1913–14, he was chosen to lead the MCC side to tour South Africa. England won the five match series by four Tests to nil, Douglas hitting his one and only Test century, 119 at Durban.

He returned to England for the 1914 season very much a hero. He continued the form he'd shown in South Africa, taking 8 for 139 against Leicestershire in the opening match, 6 for 55 against Lancashire, 74 not out and 6 for 60 in the first innings against Surrey and then 5 for 38 in the second. It was during this game, that he bowled the great Jack Hobbs twice – Hobbs always considered Douglas one of the best bowlers he ever faced. He took 9 for 62 in the match against Derbyshire and represented the Gentlemen against the Players at Lord's, taking 9 for 105 and 4 for 67. In his ten matches for the Gentlemen in those fixtures at Lord's, he took 42 wickets at a cost of 18.70 runs each. He had a superb season in 1914, scoring 1,151 runs and taking 118 wickets. He was the first Essex player to do the 'double' and not surprisingly, he was named as one of Wisden's 'Five Cricketers of the Year'.

During the war, he attained the rank of Lieut-Colonel in the Bedfordshire Regiment, developing a military-like manner, which concealed his generous nature.

Douglas never knew the meaning of defeat, showing this to the full in the magnificent win over champions Middlesex at Leyton in 1920. Essex batting first could only muster 133, Middlesex replying with 212. In their second innings, Essex scored 196, leaving Middlesex 118 to win. The task seemed a formality, but Douglas, bowling with great, tenacity had the first six Middlesex batsman back in the pavilion with the score on 33. Middlesex rallied with Plum Warner in his last season at the helm. With Warner on 46 and Middlesex just five short of victory, Douglas bowled the perfect yorker to bowl him and take Essex to a remarkable four run win.

In 1921, Douglas turned in some remarkable performances with both bat and ball. Against Worcestershire, he hit 123 not out and had match figures of 14 for 156. At the end of May that summer,

Douglas had an outstanding match against Derbyshire, turning in his career best with both bat and ball, 210 not out and 9 for 47. The Essex side finished third from bottom in the championship table that season, only winning five of its matches, yet Douglas' performances in those games was outstanding:

Inns	No's	Runs	H.Sc.	Average
7	3	562	210*	140.50

Ovrs	Mdns	Runs	Wkts	Average
202.3	48	516	53	9.76

In 1923 Douglas hit 147 not out against Gloucestershire as he and Jack O'Connor put on 206 for the sixth wicket. Their stand had been equalled, but never beaten as a County record. He was the most successful bowler in 1922 with 102 wickets, including 8 for 45 at Cheltenham in the match with Gloucestershire.

He completed the 'double' the following season, taking 146 wickets, including a hat-trick against Sussex at Leyton; his victims being Tate, Bowley and Cook.

Over the next few seasons Douglas struggled to produce anything like his best form, but wouldn't admit that anything was wrong with him. The problem was eventually diagnosed as appendicitis and he was operated on. His bowling was never quite the same: afterwards he was always struggling for both pace and swerve.

By 1927 he had returned to something like his old self. His bowling had lost its zip, but his batting had changed into something of a more aggressive nature and he once again topped the 1,000 run mark. His final century in a first-class game came in September 1927, whilst appearing for the MCC against Yorkshire at Scarborough.

At the end of the 1928 season, the Essex Committee suggested to Douglas that he should resign as captain. He refused and fought the Committee as he had fought his battles on the cricket field, in what was a protracted and sad business. He was invited to become a member of the selection committee and to play as often as possible for Essex – he did neither.

In 1930, Douglas was drowned when returning home from a business trip whilst unsuccessfully attempting to save his father, after their steamship the Oberon had collided wth another, the Arcturus, in the dense fog of the North Sea near Laeso, Denmark.

His end with the county was a sad one, but Johnny Douglas had given his life to Essex cricket. He had carried the county for 18 years (only W.G. has led a county for a longer period) and his own performances had brought great honour to the Club. The debt that Essex cricket owes to him is one that can never be repaid.

RAY EAST

Born: 20 June 1947, Manningtree
Played: 1965–1984

FIRST-CLASS ESSEX RECORDS

Matches	Innings	NO	Runs	HS	Avge	100s
405	513	111	7,103	113	17.66	1

Runs	Wkts	Avge	BB	5wl	10wm	Ct
25,804	1,010	25.54	8/30	49	10	251

TEST MATCHES – 0

It was Peter Smith who persuaded the East family that Ray at the age of sixteen, possessed a talent that made professional cricket a suitable career to pursue. His early preparation for the first-class game mostly involved playing for the Suffolk village of Brantham.

By 1965, after two seasons with the 2nd XI, he made his first-class debut for Essex against Oxford University. Against Gloucestershire at Ilford the following season (it was his third county championship match) he took nine wickets in the match, five of them caught and bowled. He impressed in both championship and one-day fixtures, where one of his early successes was to take 5 for 15 against Worcestershire in the John Player League.

In 1968 in the championship match with Warwickshire at Leyton, he took 15 for 115 in the match: his best overall bowling figures. The following summer saw him have match figures of 8 for 68 when Essex beat the New Zealanders by 15 runs at Westcliff. It was during this 1969 season that he turned in two remarkable bowling performances in the John Player League, taking 5 for 18 against Worcestershire at Harlow and 6 for 18 against Yorkshire at Hull.

His batting had been improving steadily over the seasons and in 1972 with Worcestershire once again the opponents, he scored 89 not out in the fixture at Leyton. He was involved in two useful one-day batting partnerships; he helped put on 67 for the ninth wicket with Stuart Turner in the Gillette Cup match with Gloucestershire at Chelmsford and an undefeated stand of 25 with John Lever in the John Player League against Glamorgan at Ebbw Vale – both of these came in 1973. In fact, he and Stuart Turner in 1982 set a new tenth wicket partnership record in the Nat West Trophy, putting on 81 against Yorkshire at Headingley.

Ray East turned the ball a great deal and once performed the hat-trick in a Test trial. His feat however was unrewarded, and he never won a place in the England side. He did in the 1973–74 close season, tour South Africa with the D H Robbins XI.

His one and only first-class hundred was made in 1976 when Essex entertained Hampshire at Chelmsford, East making 113.

In 1977, Ray East was instrumental in Essex gaining their first victory of the season. It came at Ilford at the end of May with Nottinghamshire the opposition. East took 4 for 71 and 8 for 30, the best figures of his career, Essex winning by six wickets. His performance in the Nottinghamshire second innings was the best recorded by any bowler that summer. He took 73 first-class wickets that season, with a week at Leyton in August the most memorable of the season. In only 45 minutes play (which was all that was possible on the first two days) he took 8 Derbyshire wickets for 57. In the second game that week, he demolished Glamorgan, taking 8 for 90 and 4 for 23.

His best season was 1978, when he took 92 wickets – it was his benefit year. During 1980–81 he played for an Overseas XI against Board Presidents XI at Calcutta. In 1981, he and David Acfield destroyed Kent at Canterbury, Acfield taking the honours in the first innings, but East returning figures of 7 for 49 in Kent's second innings as Essex won by 140 runs. In the return match at Chelmsford, Essex won by an innings, East returning match figures of 12 for 123.

In 1983, Ray East bowled 40.1 overs against Hampshire in their second innings of the match at Southend, taking 3 for 161, thus reaching 1,000 wickets in first-class cricket. When recalled to the county side in 1984, following David Acfield's injury, he took 10 wickets in his four matches, enabling him to take his tally to 1,010. Ray has taken five wickets in an innings against every county except Sussex. At the end of the 1984 season, Ray East became coach and 2nd XI captain, succeeding Mike Denness.

Ray's humorous exploits are quite legendary such as the time he was brought on at the end of the day by Keith Fletcher after the seamers had bowled all morning and afternoon. His reaction was to cup his hands and yell out 'East' towards the scorers as if they had called for the bowler's name, as they often do in club cricket when an unknown bowler appears. On one occasion when several Essex players went down with a 'flu virus, he walked up and down in front of the dressing room with a placard marked 'UNCLEAN'. Legendary they may be, but they often hid the fact that he was one of only nine Essex bowlers to have taken more than 1,000 wickets for the county.

LAWRIE EASTMAN

Born: 3 June 1897, Enfield
Died: 17 April 1941
Played: 1920–1939

FIRST-CLASS ESSEX RECORDS

Matches	Innings	NO	Runs	HS	Avge	100s
442	679	49	12,965	161	20.57	7

Runs	Wkts	Avge	BB	5wI	10wm	Ct
26,102	975	26.77	7/28	29	3	254

TEST MATCHES – 0

Lawrence Charles Eastman was originally an amateur player whose ambition to take up medicine as a profession had been thwarted by the war, during which he won the DCM and MM. He turned professional in 1927. His love for the game of cricket had been noticed by Johnny Douglas and Percy Perrin and so he was invited to play for the county in their match against Gloucestershire at Bristol. It was a game marred by rain, but Eastman's medium-pace bowling brought him figures of 5 for 53, including a spell of three wickets in four balls. The following game at Lord's, Eastman went in at number 10, hitting a superb 91 after Russell had scored a century. In fact, the pair added 175 before the stumps were drawn for the day and went on to record what was at the time a ninth wicket record stand of 184.

In his early years with the county, he was greatly helped in his development by Essex stalwarts, Douglas, McGahey, Perrin and Russell.

During the 1922 season, he took 57 wickets, including 7 for 28 (his best analysis) in the match against Somerset at Taunton. His best match figures of 12 for 82 came in the match against Sussex at Leyton; also in this match, he went in at number 10 and hit an unbeaten 37. This was also the year that Eastman was appointed assistant-secretary at Leyton and became a regular member of the county team.

In 1924, Eastman hit his maiden century against Surrey at Southend and at the initial first-class game to be played at Chelmsford in 1925, he hit 93 against Oxford University.

He was now developing into a hard-hitting opening batsman. He never hesitated to use the straight drive, which when executed properly, brought him six runs and he could also hook well. In 1925 at Leyton in the match against Lancashire, he and Cutmore made opening stands of 115 and 172. His highest score came four years later in 1929, when he hit 161 against Derbyshire at Derby. He exceeded 700 runs and 50 wickets in 1925, his all-round talents beginning to flourish. The following season he took 6 for 59 in the tied match against Somerset at Chelmsford.

In his early days, Eastman bowled medium-pace, but served Essex best when he changed to spin. He could turn the ball both ways but was particularly deadly with the leg-break. Against Somerset at Weston-super-Mare in 1934, his first innings bowling analysis was 4 wickets for 0 runs. He ended the West Country side's innings in just thirteen deliveries, dismissing Bennett, Hazell, Ingle and Wellard.

Lancashire arrived at Chelmsford in 1935 as the reigning county champions, but were easily beaten by ten wickets. In their second innings, the red-rose side were dismissed for 83, Eastman taking 3 for 4.

In 1937 he scored 86 against Glamorgan at Westcliff, hitting 5 sixes and 12 fours – all but eight of his runs coming from boundaries.

During the 1939 season, Eastman's bowling tended to fall away, but he had a good summer with the bat, scoring 1,027 runs at an average of 26.33. In the match against Surrey at Colchester, he was cruelly run out for 99. Eastman had once commented that he had batted in every position except number 11. In his benefit match at Southend, when Middlesex were the visitors, he was forced to bat last, due to him having water on the knee. Essex unfortunately lost the game by five runs – if Eastman hadn't been injured they most surely would have won. His benefit match realised £1,200 – quite a sum in those days, for Eastman was a popular all-rounder.

Eastman paid three visits as coach to New Zealand as well as having a spell coaching at Kimberley, South Africa. In 1937 he was a member of the team which toured the Argentine.

He didn't enjoy the best of health for quite a few years, otherwise there is no doubt he would have been seen to much greater advantage on the cricket field. When the war broke out, Eastman helped the London counties and was especially proud of being captain when the side first appeared at Lord's. During the Second World War Eastman worked as an ARP warden. Whilst performing his duties he was almost hit by a high-explosive bomb, causing severe shock. He died at Harefield Sanatorium on 17 April 1941, following an operation.

The Essex Committee did their utmost to arrange a benefit match against the London Counties for Lawrie Eastman's widow. Unfortunately, due to the problems of finding a ground and organisation, the proposal had to be dropped. It was a great shame, for Lawrie Eastman was only 43 years old and had played for the county from 1920 until 1939.

BRIAN EDMEADES

Born: 17 September 1941, Matlock
Played: 1961–1976

FIRST-CLASS ESSEX RECORDS

Matches	Innings	NO	Runs	HS	Avge	100s
335	555	69	12,593	163	25.91	14

Runs	Wkts	Avge	BB	5wl	10wm	Ct
9,688	374	25.90	7/37	10	1	105

TEST MATCHES – 0

Brian Edmeades, though born in Matlock, Derbyshire was in all other departments an East Londoner. He had played for both London and Essex schoolboys in representative cricket and was also a good footballer. However, in the summer months, he was scoring runs and steadily picking up wickets as a change bowler, a performance noted by Essex coach Frank Rist. When he was ready to leave school, Essex offered him a trial. There appeared to be no chance for him at the Ilford nets, as the hopeful young cricketers batted and bowled, yet when the nets emptied, he was the only one to be offered a staff position.

He made his first-class debut for Essex against South African Fezela at Chelmsford in June 1961, playing his first county game against Surrey the following month.

In 1963 Edmeades had a good match against Gloucestershire at Leyton. Essex were 67 for 8 when Edmeades was joined by Paddy Phelan. They put on 93 for the ninth wicket, Edmeades scoring 44. Despite this, Essex ended 37 behind on the first innings and it was only a knock of 80 by Trevor Bailey and good bowling by Brian Edmeades (4 for 23) that saw Essex the winners by 68 runs.

In 1964 Essex defeated the Australians at Southend, Edmeades scoring an unbeaten 53 as the county totalled 425 for 6. This was also the season that Brian Edmeades scored his maiden first-class century. Batting at number 3, he scored 135 in the match against Lancashire at Old Trafford, before being bowled by Brian Statham. A sound batsman, he had his most successful season so far. Coupled with his medium-pace bowling and great outfielding, he was a great favourite with the Essex crowds.

In 1965 he took 3 for 36 in Derbyshire's first innings and 7 for 43 in the second, as Essex ran out worthy winners by 85 runs. It was the only time he took ten wickets in a match. At the end of the season, he was awarded his county cap.

In 1966 Edmeades was without doubt, the outstanding bowler for Essex. He bowled 725 overs and took 106 wickets at an average of 18.59 runs apiece. It is a little unkind to say, but he was helped by the rule that the first innings in championship games was restricted to 65 overs per side, resulting as with all over-limitation games in a mad scramble for runs from middle-order batsmen and a harvest of wickets for seam bowlers. He headed the Essex bowling averages that summer and produced the best figures of his career, 7 for 37 against Glamorgan at Leyton. In fact, he took four or more wickets in an innings on eleven occasions. He took 4 for 20 as Nottinghamshire were defeated by 56 runs. Kent were beaten by just four runs at Dartford, Edmeades having match figures of 9 for 84 (5 for 55 and 4 for 29). He also took 3 for 32 against Derbyshire at Chesterfield, as Essex recorded their first win against a Championship side in the Gillette Cup.

Brian Edmeades had the nickname amongst his Essex team-mates of 'Chanson' – a result of him continually playing 'Chanson d'Amour' when in cafés possessing a juke box!

As the years went by, Edmeades began to establish himself as one of the most consistent opening batsmen on the county circuit. When Brian Taylor took over as captain, one of his first moves was to move the most successful bowler of 1966 to bat at number 3 in 1967. He applied his professionalism and scored over a thousand runs.

In 1970 Essex beat the reigning county champions, Kent at Tunbridge Wells. He shared in a first wicket stand of 98 with Taylor and a similar second wicket stand with Saville, Edmeades contribution being 80 runs. This was his best season, Edmeades scoring 1,620 runs at an average of 35.21.

Edmeades missed the beginning of the 1971 season with an eye injury, but returned with a vengeance the following season to hit the highest score of his career, 163 against Leicestershire at Leyton. His career ended with him as an attacking opening batsman, but his medium-paced bowling ensured that he played a vital part in any match, especially the one-day game. In 1973, he took 5 for 22 against Leicestershire at Ilford in the Benson & Hedges Cup. In 1976 he hit 125 not out in sharing a second wicket record in the Benson and Hedges Cup of 172 with Ken McEwan against Minor Counties (East) at Norwich. At the end of the 1976 season, Edmeades announced his retirement to take up an appointment in Scotland. He had served the county well for 16 seasons, but continued to play professionally for five years with Clydesdale, his career ending in 1981 when he felt his eyesight and elbows could no longer stand up to the requirements of the game. Yet with Clydesdale, he won cups and leagues that had eluded him with Essex.

Brian Edmeades was a great favourite with Essex crowds, for he was always in the game. He was an all-rounder whose exciting approach to the game typified the county who specialised in all-rounders.

FREDERICK FANE

Born: 27 April 1875, Curragh Camp, Ireland
Died: 27 November 1960
Played: 1895–1922

FIRST-CLASS ESSEX RECORDS

Matches	Innings	NO	Runs	HS	Avge	100s
292	512	30	12,599	217	26.13	18

Runs	Wkts	Avge	BB	5wl	10wm	Ct
32	0	:::::	–	–	–	141

TEST MATCHES – 14

Frederick Luther Fane was born on 27 April 1875 at Curragh Camp, where his father F.J. Fane (who played for both Ireland and Essex in pre-first-class days) was serving with his regiment.

From 1892–94, Frederick Fane spent three years in the Charterhouse XI before moving on to Oxford. He never d d himself justice at Oxford, failing to get his Blue as a freshman, failing in both his Varsity match appearances and only reaching 50 once during his time there.

He made his Essex debut in 1895 in the match against Somerset at Leyton. It was Essex's first win on this ground, Fane making a promising start with 36, after he and 'Bob' Carpenter had scored 46 in the first 35 minutes.

In 1899, Fane scored 207 against Leicestershire at Grace Road, the first double century to be hit for Essex. In 1901, he shared in an undefeated stand of 235 with Percy Perrin in the match against Nottinghamshire at Leyton, as Essex finished 27 runs short of victory.

Fane succeeded Charles Kortright as Essex captain in 1904. He came to the post at a very difficult time. The County Club had narrowly avoided liquidation and the nucleus of their bowling attack would not be playing. Fane was unusual in that although he captained both Essex and England, he was a reluctant captain who undertook the task with considerable reservations.

Fane was an attractive, front-footed batsman, who liked nothing better than to open the innings. His footwork was nimble and he could quickly get down the wicket to the pitch of the ball. Fane could also be a very attractive batsman to watch. He was a good deep fielder and had a safe pair of hands, a fact which may well have influenced his dislike of captaincy.

In 1902–03 he toured New Zealand and Australia as a member of Lord Hawke's side (captained by Plum Warner), scoring over 500 runs with a brilliant hundred against New Zealand at Christchurch. In 1905–06, he went to South Africa under Warner and headed the batting averages with 607 runs at an average of 37.93. Fane was one of the few members of the side to adjust to the matting pitches and the opposing leg-break and googly attack. He hit fifties in the second and fourth Test matches and a magnificent 143 at Johannesburg in the third Test.

In 1906 his third and last year of captaincy with Essex, he was rewarded with the county finishing in seventh place in the championship with nine victories. At Leyton, when Middlesex were the opponents, Fane and Douglas opened with a stand of 208. It was his best season, Fane scoring 1,572 runs at an average of 34.93. He decided to resign as captain because of his inability to commit himself to play on a regular basis.

In 1907–08, he was a member of the MCC side under A O Jones which toured Australia. He scored 133 in the first match at Perth and, when Jones was taken ill, it was Fane who took over the captaincy for the first two Tests. He was the first Essex cricketer to captain his country. In the first Test, he took an unpopular decision – this was to include George Gunn, who had accompanied the team for health reasons and usually acted as scorer in preference to a promising young Surrey player by the name of Jack Hobbs! Gunn didn't let his captain down, scoring 119 and 74. Fane went on another tour to South Africa and in all, represented his country on 14 occasions, scoring 682 runs at an average of 26.23, but he never played for England at home.

In 1908, he and Douglas in another long opening stand, made 207 against Kent at Leyton. In 1909, Essex drew both games against the Australian tourists, with Fane hitting a masterly 15 in the first encounter. In 1911, Fane hit 217 against Surrey at the Oval. This was the top score made by an Essex batsman that summer and was his highest career score. His innings took five-and-a-quarter hours, the future Kings Edward VIII and George VI being among the spectators. He followed this with 162 against Sussex at Eastbourne, but the county lost the game by 119 runs.

On the outbreak of the First World War, despite being almost 40, he enlisted almost immediately and on 13 October 1914 was commissioned into the Leeds Rifles. It was a good choice, as I'm sure he was well aware, for it was a cricketing battalion, raised and commanded by the ex-England captain, Hon. F S Jackson. In April 1917, the Leeds Rifles were ordered to push forward towards the Hindenburg Line as part of an overall plan which later became the first battle of Bullecourt. It was during this time that Fane distinguished himself and in June was awarded the Military Cross.

When the war was over, Fane made only spasmodic appearances for Essex, his last coming in 1922 and two years later, he played his last first-class match.

In 1938, at the ripe old age of 63, he got married and had two daughters, the younger being born when Fane was 77. He died in 1960, at the age of 85, though in 1956, due to an editorial error he had read his obituary in Wisden, it having been wrongly inserted in mistake for his cousin.

KEN FARNES

Born: 8 July, Leytonstone
Died: 20 October 1941
Played: 1930–1939

FIRST-CLASS ESSEX RECORDS

Matches	Innings	NO	Runs	HS	Avge	100s
79	94	31	590	97*	9.36	–

Runs	Wkts	Avge	BB	5wl	10wm	Ct
7,086	367	19.30	8/38	28	5	42

TEST MATCHES – 16

Kenneth Farnes arrived in the Essex side via Romford's Royal Liberty School, where he owed much to the encouragement given him by the headmaster, Mr. S.B. Hartley, a great cricket enthusiast and the Gidea Park Club, where he'd been spotted by Percy Perrin playing against the Essex Club and Ground.

He made his Essex debut in 1930 against Gloucestershire at Chelmsford, failing to take a wicket, but in his next match against

Kent at Southend, he took 5 for 36 in 17 overs. One of his victims was the great Frank Woolley, who went for nought, brilliantly taken by Jack Russell at second slip; his other victims in this impressive spell included Les Ames and 'Tich' Freeman, two great players. In 1930, he went up to Pembroke College, Cambridge, winning a Blue as a freshman the following year. He gained further blues in 1932 and 1933.

In 1931, he took 6 for 57 against Lancashire, this being the first game played at the Vista Road Ground, Clacton – Essex winning by an innings and 64 runs.

He played in a Test trial in 1932 and was a serious contender for a place on the infamous 'body-line' tour to Australia in 1932–33. His work for Cambridge showed 41 wickets at 17.39 runs apiece. At the end of the 1933 University term, he arrived to play for Essex, going on to take 67 wickets in the championship at a cost of 16.07 runs each in the ten matches he played. There can be no doubt about it, he was the most effective amateur bowler in the country. His best performance was 7 for 21 against Surrey at Southend, also taking 13 for 98 in the match against Somerset at Taunton.

Ken Farnes was a tall, lively fast bowler. Standing at 6ft 5½ins and weighing 15½ stone, he had a superb action. His run was short, 11 strides, but he could move the ball both ways, bringing it down from such a great height that he was able to get it to lift sharply off the pitch, making it difficult for batsmen to time their strokes.

Farnes was the outstanding bowler of the 1934 season, taking 37 County Championship wickets at a cost of 16.40 runs – this in just 13 innings. He was in terrific form against Yorkshire at Southend, taking 7 for 59 in their second innings and 11 wickets in the match. He also made his Test debut this summer against Australia at Trent Bridge, taking 5 wickets in each innings. He thus became the third England bowler after F Martin and T Richardson to take 10 wickets in his first Test against Australia.

He missed much of the 1935 season through injury, but returned the following summer to take 61 wickets in 11 County Championship matches. Probably his greatest spell of fast bowling was in the Gentlemen v Players match at Lord's – he clean bowled Gimblett, Hammond and Hardstaff, the stump being knocked head high before landing at the wicket-keeper's feet. Also in 1936, he contributed 97 not out to Essex's 10th wicket stand of 149 with Tommy Wade against Somerset at Taunton. He was chosen to tour Australia in the winter of 1936–37 with Gubby Allen's side.

It was in this series that he produced his best Test bowling figures of 6 for 96, in Australia's total of 604 in perfect batting conditions.

In the 1937 season he took 5 for 65 when representing the Gentlemen in their match against the Players, but then suffered a strain which kept him out of the third Test match against New Zealand.

In 1938 Kenneth Farnes was back to his best form. He took 56 championship wickets at a cost of 14.89 runs each. In all the matches that summer he took 107 wickets at 18.84 runs apiece. He played in four Tests against the Australians that year, taking 13 wickets. He also represented the Gentlemen against the Players at Lord's, taking 8 for 43 in the Players' first innings. He turned in other good returns in that season, including 15 for 113 against Glamorgan at Clacton and 14 for 119 against Worcestershire at New Road. That season also saw him chosen as one of Wisden's 'Five Cricketers of the Year'. He was asked to join the tour party to South Africa that coming winter.

For three seasons he formed a devastating partnership with 'Hopper' Read, which was the fastest in England.

In 1939, Farnes could only play from August, yet he still took 33 wickets in the championship at 18.57 runs each. He performed his only hat-trick against Nottinghamshire at Clacton, taking 5 for 30 in the process; his victims being Heane, Hardstaff Junior and Gunn. In the second match of the Clacton Festival, he took 6 for 47 against Northamptonshire.

In 1940, Kenneth Farnes joined the RAF and was sent to do his training in Canada. He returned home to become a night-flying pilot and within four weeks of his return to England he was killed when the plane in which he was pilot crashed. It was the night of 20 October 1941, he was only 30 years of age. His death was a great blow to both Essex and England cricket.

In June 1954, a memorial in the shape of a score-board at Gidea Park Ground, Romford was dedicated by the Bishop of Chelmsford to Kenneth Farnes, one of the fastest bowlers of all time and the leading amateur bowler of the 1930s.

Kenneth C. Preston

Michael J. Bear

Gordon Barker

Thomas H. Wade

Thomas P. B. Smith

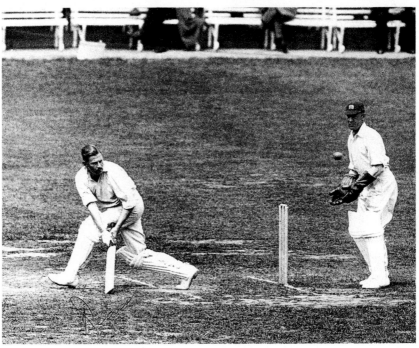

Thomas N. Pearce

Ken Farnes

Frank H. Vigar

Thomas C. Dodds

WilliamT. Greensmith

Barry R. Knight

Brian Taylor

Robin N. S. Hobbs

Brian E. A. Edmeades

Keith W. R. Fletcher

Stuart Turner

David L. Acfield

John K. Lever

Ray E. East

Keith D. Boyce

Brian R. Hardie

Ken S. McEwan

Norbert Phillip

Derek R. Pringle

Neil A. Foster

Graham A. Gooch

KEITH FLETCHER

Born: 20 May 1944, Worcester
Played: 1962–1989

FIRST-CLASS ESSEX RECORDS

Matches	Innings	NO	Runs	HS	Avge	100s
572	916	122	29,374	228*	36.99	45

Runs	Wkts	Avge	BB	5wl	10wm	Ct
1,268	29	43.72	5/41	1	–	517

TEST MATCHES – 59

Keith William Robert Fletcher was born in Worcester but at the age of four moved with his family to the Cambridgeshire village of Caldecote. Unlike most young cricket professionals, he never played cricket for the village schools at Bourne and later Comberton because there were rarely enough boys to make a team. His cricket was really a development of natural talent fostered in the nets of the Caldecote village team, where his father did his best to pass on his knowledge of the game. His batting soon had the village cricketers wondering whether an eleven year old boy was too young to risk – they took what was a calculated gamble and just after his eleventh birthday, this boy prodigy made his debut. At the age of 13, he joined Royston to get more cricket experience and at the same time, he was recommended to Essex by his headteacher, who suggested they take a look at him.

The result was that he began playing for Essex Young Amateurs at the age of 14. A careers officer visiting his school was startled to hear that Keith wanted to become a professional cricketer. He took the time to inform Harry Crabtree (the Sports Education Officer for Essex). He informed Trevor Bailey and he arranged for Keith to play in an Essex Club and Ground match against Colchester and East Essex, after which he was signed on at the age of 16. When he arrived to join the staff, some of the players were practising close catching and noticing his long and rather pointed shoes, they promptly nicknamed him the 'Gnome'.

He made his first team debut in 1962, having only seen one first-class cricket match. The following season, he began to show his attractive batting skills and scored 1,310 runs at an average of 26.20. He was rewarded with his cap, though the undoubted potential of his cricket had yet to be fulfilled. Essex encountered the mighty West Indies that summer at Southend, the match being drawn, and it was Keith Fletcher with an innings of 29 from an Essex total of 56 who just averted the follow on and who was the top scorer in the Essex second innings with 34 not out.

When Essex beat the Australians at Southend in 1964, Fletcher scored 125 before being bowled by Bob Cowper. His maiden century came when he hit 103 not out against Lancashire at Old Trafford that season, going on to score 1,616 runs at an average of 31.07. In 1965, he totalled 1,486 runs at an average of 29.13, yet the following summer he scored 1,550 runs, including a superb 106 against the West Indies at Southend. There was certainly no uncertainty in the nineties, as he picked up a glorious six down the leg side off Wes Hall and then drove another off Conrad Hunte to take him to his hundred.

In 1966, he took 42 catches during the season, breaking his own record from the previous season. In 1967, he took six catches in the match against Glamorgan at Brentwood, performing the feat on two further occasions against Worcestershire and Derbyshire in 1977 and 1978 respectively.

Like many batsmen, he was rightly proud of the day that his leg-spinning reached its peak. It came at Peshawar in 1966–67 when he took 4 for 50 for the MCC Under-25 team.

He hit the highest score of his career, 228 not out against Sussex at Hastings in 1968 and then in June that season, he made 131 not out at Bath against Somerset, an innings full of aggressive stroke making which was one of the knocks that gained him his first England cap. It came at Headingley that summer and for the wrong reasons. He will never forget it. He had been named in the England twelve but it wasn't expected that he would play. However, Tom Graveney cut his hand opening a can of food and Yorkshire's Phil Sharpe, who hadn't even been in the original squad was called up as standby. It was quite natural that Fletcher should play, but of course the Yorkshire crowd saw it differently – they thought Sharpe should play and as Fletcher dropped three catches and made nought, the Leeds crowd never let up.

Against Glamorgan at Chelmsford in 1971, Fletcher hit an unbeaten 164. He went on to finish second to Geoff Boycott in the national batting averages. In 1972, Fletcher's form was outstanding; it amazed most Essex followers that he was only chosen for one Test that summer. Against Yorkshire, he made a brilliant 139 not out (four sixes and 12 fours) to clinch an Essex victory. He played another fine innings of 181 not out against Glamorgan that summer. Essex facing a Glamorgan total of 338 for 9 declared, were looking for bonus points. They declared at 350 for 1, after Fletcher and Graham Saville had added 288 in ten minutes short of three hours. Fletcher hit four sixes and 24 fours, as Essex went on to win the match.

In 1973, his innings of 178 against New Zealand at Lord's averted England's first defeat by New Zealand.

At the end of the 1973 season he was appointed captain in succession to Brian Taylor. Fletcher was a firm disciplinarian, earning great respect from the players because of his own natural ability. At the end of his first season in charge he was chosen as one of Wisden's 'Five Cricketers of the Year'. It proved a difficult year from his own viewpoint as his appearances in the England test team meant frequent absences from Essex.

His century against Pakistan at the Oval in 1974 ramains the slowest (458 minutes) in English first-class cricket.

In 1976, he hit a century in each innings, 111 and 102 not out in the match against Nottinghamshire at Trent Bridge.

In 1979, Fletcher hit 140 not out in the win over Derbyshire at Chesterfield – it was his first century for Essex for two years. It was just the start Fletcher needed, going on to pass 1,000 runs for the season and taking Essex to their first County Championship trophy success. He also produced his career best bowling figures this season, taking 5 for 41 in the defeat by Middlesex at Colchester.

In 1981 Fletcher passed the 1,000 run mark, hitting 123 not out against Warwickshire and an unbeaten 165 against Kent at Chelmsford. By the end of that summer, more and more people were beginning to sit up and take notice of Keith Fletcher and Essex. His leadership qualities prompted the England Committee to name him captain of the England party to tour India and Sri Lanka in 1981–82. He was the third Essex player to captain his country. Keith Fletcher was the only England captain to win the toss 5 times in a 6 – Test series and the first England captain to put the opposition in first in India.

He played in 59 Tests for England, 7 of them as captain. He hit 7 centuries, the highest being 216 against New Zealand at Auckland in 1974–75, but probably his best Test innings was the 170 also made aginst New Zealand at Lord's in 1973.

After returning from the 1981–82 tour of India and Sri Lanka, he was relieved of the captaincy, because it was felt that he couldn't earn his place in the side purely as a batsman. He then proceeded to hit 120 at Lord's against Middlesex in the first game of the season, following it with another century, 122 against Surrey two games later. He also took 101 off the Sussex attack at Hove in a Benson and Hedges cup zonal match. In fact, he only just fell short of making centuries in the other one-day competitions, scoring 99 not out against Nottinghamshire in the 1974 John Player League and 97 against Kent in the 1982 Nat West Bank Trophy.

In 1982, his testimonial raised £83,250, following on from the £13,000 his benefit brought him some nine years earlier.

In 1983, Fletcher took a hundred off Glamorgan in a rain-affected match at Cardiff and 110 in the game against Surrey at Chelmsford. In 1984, in a game I remember well, Essex asked Lancashire to bat first in the game at Old Trafford. Lancashire scored 229, then Essex scored at a remarkable rate and ended up with 446. Essex then dismissed Lancashire for the same score as in their first innings and then knocked off the required runs to win inside two days – Fletcher was a .happy man! Essex were the champions for the second year running.

In 1985, Fletcher was invited to Buckingham Palace to receive the OBE from Her Majesty The Queen. It was an honour thoroughly and richly deserved, reflecting the fortunes of both the man and the County Club. By the end of that season, Keith Fletcher had become the first captain to have led a county side to the game's four major honours, his side having won the John Player League and the Nat West Bank Trophy. At the end of that summer, he stood down as captain to enable Graham Gooch to gain experience and to offer advice and take over when Gooch was absent on test duty.

Keith Fletcher was an exciting and talented middle-order batsman, playing his last game for Essex in 1989. He has scored more first-class runs for Essex than any other batsman and possessed a shrewd cricket brain and was a skilful leader of men. There have been few greater servants to the County Club than the 'Gnome'.

NEIL FOSTER

Born: 6 May 1962, Colchester
Played: 1980–

FIRST-CLASS ESSEX RECORDS

Matches	Innings	NO	Runs	HS	Avge	100s
138	152	37	2,381	101	20.70	1

Runs	Wkts	Avge	BB	5wl	10wm	Ct
13,979	599	23.33	7/33	34	6	60

TEST MATCHES – 28

On 6 May 1980, Neil Foster was celebrating his 18th birthday in Colchester, by preparing for his 'A' Levels at the Philip Morant

Comprehensive School. He had just signed forms for Essex and was no doubt wondering how the Essex side were doing in their match with Somerset at Ilford, as a virus was decimating the team. Such was Essex's plight that Neil Foster was called to the headteacher's office to be told that he had been included in the side for his first-class debut the following day against Kent.

Kent won the toss and elected to bat. Foster, opening the bowling with John Lever, sent his first delivery racing away for four wides. In successive overs, he claimed the wickets of England internationals Bob Woolmer and Chris Tavare and later Alan Ealham to finish with figures of 15 – 3 – 51 – 3.

In 1981 he played for Young England against Young India. In 1982, playing in his fifth Championship match of the summer against Lancashire at Aigburth, he was experiencing pain in his back, diagnosed to be a stress fracture of a vertebra. He tried to cure the problem the same way that had been successful for Dennis Lillee, by spending time encased in a plaster corset. Unfortunately for him it didn't work and he had to resort to surgery for the insertion of steel plates to hold the crack together.

However, by the end of May the following season, Foster had made an amazing recovery and was in the Essex side. He was awarded his county cap this summer for some very fine fast bowling, hard-hitting and good fielding. After the first day's play of the game with Surrey had been washed out, Foster with 4 for 10 helped Phillip destroy the visitors and bowl them out for 14. When he dismissed Alan Butcher cheaply in the Surrey second innings, it looked as though a repeat performance was on the cards, but it wasn't to be. During the course of the season, he was to win his first England cap, making his Test debut against New Zealand. His first wicket for England was Jeremy Coney, Foster taking 1 for 35 in the second innings after 0 for 40 in the first. He had bowled well on his test debut, but returned to Essex to find that he couldn't play again that season due to problems with his back. It was at the end of July when Foster had to return to hospital to have a major operation which included the insertion of two metal plates to cure a damaged spine. However, by the end of the season he had rejoined his Essex team-mates and was selected to tour New Zealand and Pakistan with the England team.

In 1984, when Essex won the County Championship, Foster took 87 wickets at 24.11 runs each, with 6 for 79 his best performance.

He has a high bowling action which allows him to extract awkward bounce. When the ball is swinging he can command useful movement away from the right-hander through the air, getting close to the stumps. When the pitch is receptive to movement rather than atmosphere, he bangs it down on the seam. He has enough pace to make all the top-class batsmen hurry their shots and can still beat them for speed.

In Madras in 1984–85 in the fourth Test, he took 11 for 163, a match-winning performance, achieved in unhelpful conditions against a strong Indian batting side.

In 1985, he hit 63 in the County Championship match against Lancashire at Ilford, it remained his highest score until last season (1990). Against Surrey at the Oval in the Benson and Hedges Cup, he took 5 for 32, following it in 1986 with another five-wicket haul in a one-day match, 5 for 17 against Derbyshire in the John Player League.

He ended the 1986 season with 105 first-class wickets, producing the best match figures of his career so far in the game against Worcestershire, with 11 for 157. During the tour of Australia in 1986–87 he hit his highest score outside this country, 74 not out in the match against Queensland at Brisbane.

In 1987, he produced his best bowling figures, both in the County Championship and at Test level. He took 7 for 33 against Warwickshire at Chelmsford and 8 for 107 against Pakistan at Headingley. He has played in 28 tests taking 76 wickets at 31.26 runs apiece, reaching his fiftieth wicket in his eighteenth Test. At the end of the 1990 season, he was named as one of Wisden's 'Five Cricketers of the Year'.

In 1989–90, he was a member of the unofficial England Team that toured South Africa.

Last season (1990), he was the leading wicket-taker in the country with 94 wickets at a cost of 26.61 runs each. Derbyshire suffered most at the hands of Foster, as he took 6 for 49 at Colchester and 5 for 39 at Derby. He also captained Essex for the first time against Glamorgan at Southend, but the highlight of his season, must surely have been his maiden first-class hundred. It came against Leicestershire and came up in 83 minutes off 81 balls and contained 5 sixes and 8 fours.

JOHN FREEMAN

Born: 3 September 1883, Ladywell, Lewisham
Died: 8 August 1958
Played: 1905–1928

FIRST-CLASS ESSEX RECORDS

Matches	Innings	NO	Runs	HS	Ave	100s
336	577	56	14,507	286	27.84	26

Runs	Wkts	Av	BB	5wI	10wm	Ct	St
365	10	36.50	3/31	–	–	230	46

TEST MATCHES – 0

John Freeman was the brother of Kent's 'Tich' Freeman, a middle-order batsman, wicket-keeper and occasional right-arm medium-pace bowler. He played for the county over 23 years, but was never able to emulate his famous brother's success.

Freeman made his debut for Essex in 1905, soon making a reputation for himself as a most attractive stroke-maker. This coupled with his wicket-keeping made him a very important member of the Essex side.

In 1911, he had the unusual distinction of sharing with 'Bob' Carpenter in century partnerships in each innings of the match with Surrey at Leyton. He hit 841 runs this season at an average of 33.64, including two centuries. He had shown plenty of progress over the past two seasons and this was maintained throughout the 1913 season when he finished second in the Essex batting averages, as his adventurous style continued to excite the crowds. He had benefited from the coaching he received from 'Bob' Carpenter. The following summer was a disappointing one for Freeman, though he did share in a seventh wicket stand of 261 with Douglas in the match against Lancashire at Leyton, batting for over four and a half hours.

John Freeman returned after the war as impressive as ever. He was by this time, thirty five years old and had lost important years to the fighting. In 1919, he was at his prime, hitting exactly 1,000 runs.

In 1921 in the match against Derbyshire at Leyton, Freeman found himself to be the only professional in the Essex side that day. Later that summer, Freeman hit the highest score of his career, 286 against Northamptonshire at Northampton. It took him slightly under seven hours to reach this score, as he went on to reach 1,000 runs for the second time.

In the first first-class match to be played on what is now the County Ground at New Writtle Street, Chelmsford, Essex drew with Oxford University, the highlight being a fifth-wicket partnership of 200 between John Freeman and Percy Perrin. Whether it was with Perrin or Cutmore, Freeman often gave his side a most solid of starts.

For a man of 42 years of age, Freeman had a remarkable season in 1926, scoring 1,958 runs at an average of 41.65, hitting six centuries. Also this season, in the match against Middlesex, he and Russell scored 184 out of 203 from the bat in Essex's first innings. In the tied match with Somerset at Chelmsford in June this season, Freeman was the only batsman on either side to score two knocks of any consequence, 43 and 37 in a low scoring game.

By 1927, Freeman had given way to Lawrie Eastman's younger brother George behind the stumps and in fact, only played in one match in 1927. The following season was his last in first-class cricket for this most popular of Essex players.

PAUL GIBB

Born: 11 July 1913, Brandsby, Yorkshire
Died: 7 December 1977
Played: 1951–1956

FIRST-CLASS ESSEX RECORDS

Matches	Innings	NO	Runs	HS	Ave	100s
145	250	12	6,328	141	26.58	8

Runs	Wkts	Av	BB	5wI	10wm	Ct	St
4	0	::::::	–	–	–	273	66

TEST MATCHES – 8

Educated at St Edward's School, Oxford, Paul Antony Gibb gained a blue as a Cambridge freshman. At Cambridge, he kept wicket when S C Griffith was injured and kept his place behind the stumps. For his four University matches, he averaged 54 with the bat, making a century in his last year.

In 1935, whilst in his first year at Cambridge, he made his debut for his home county, Yorkshire. He scored 157 not out in this match against Nottinghamshire, for whom Harold Larwood and Bill Voce were the opening pair. After playing 36 times for Yorkshire as an amateur and captaining their pre-War Jamaican tour, he dropped out of first-class cricket on his return from Australia in 1947.

His engagement by Essex as a professional in 1951, marked an important step in the economic and social side of cricket history. He was the first University Blue to turn professional – there was now a narrowing of the gap between amateur and professional, resulting from post-war economic conditions. When he signed for Essex he was compelled to suspend his MCC membership.

He didn't quite manage a century on his Essex debut, but it wasn't too long before he hit 99 against Kent, quickly following it with 107 made against his former county Yorkshire at Brentwood. Paul Gibb had an impressive first season for Essex, scoring 1,330 runs and hitting four centuries. He also proved a more than capable successor to Tommy Wade behind the stumps. One of his best hundreds that summer came in the high scoring match against Nottinghamshire at Clacton. Nottinghamshire scored 576 for 9 declared, but Essex passed their total to secure first innings points, Paul Gibb scoring 118. When Essex played Kent at Blackheath, Gibb and his partner Horsfall, put on 343 for the third wicket – it was a new Essex record. Gibb scored 141 and along with Horsfall was later presented with a scorecard printed on silk to commemorate this record.

In 1952, Gibb scored 1,519 runs, including a share in a new second wicket stand for Essex. It came in the match against Northamptonshire, when he and Avery put on 294, Gibb hitting 132. His aggregate of victims behind the stumps, 87, put him at the head of English wicket-keepers this summer – 83 of these were for Essex, 66 being caught and 17 stumped. His best performance was against Kent at Tunbridge Wells, when he made 8 dismissals.

He once again passed the 1,000 run mark in 1953, but the following season was hampered by injuries.

In 1955 he returned to once again complete another 1,000 runs for Essex. In 1956, he still kept wicket well, but it was becoming apparent that his injuries from previous seasons were making themselves felt and he retired at the end of that season.

He represented England on eight occasions and had a batting average of 44.69. In his first Test against South Africa he scored 93 and 106 and in his final Test of that series he made 120.

He favoured playing off the back foot and was a strong resolute batsman with a good defence – his powers of concentration and patience being second to none. Paul Gibb had an enormous appetite with a special liking for ice cream, yet his slender figure was never affected by the large amount of food he ate. He used to travel the county circuit in a small van – this contained most of his belongings and was often his sleeping accommodation. On his retirement from first-class cricket he became a first-class umpire, a position he held from 1957–66.

In 1977 he was invited to the Centenary Test at Melbourne where he appeared wearing a wig and contact lenses and went unrecognized by his many former colleagues. At the time of his death he was a bus driver in Guildford.

A slight, bespectacled figure, there can be no doubt, he was a great asset to the Essex side.

GRAHAM GOOCH

Born: 23 July 1953, Leytonstone
Played: 1973–

FIRST-CLASS ESSEX RECORDS

Matches	Innings	NO	Runs	HS	Ave	100s
289	476	41	20,921	275	48.09	58

Runs	Wkts	Ave	BB	5wI	10wm	Ct
5,676	177	32.06	7/14	3	–	278

TEST MATCHES – 81

Beginning at Norlington Junior High School, Leytonstone, Graham Gooch played in all the representative teams available to him on his way into the Essex side. When he was first invited to join the Essex staff, he decided that he should become a qualified tradesman, so for the first few years, he played for the Club and Ground and 2nd XI, when he could take leave from his work as an apprentice toolmaker. In fact, when he first joined Essex, he was a batsman who kept wicket and actually went on a Young England tour to the West Indies as Number 2 wicket-keeper to Gloucestershire's Andy Stovold.

He made his first-team debut in 1973, playing in just one Championship match. It wasn't until the beginning of June the following season that he began to make his mark. His first game that season was at Bristol against Gloucestershire, where he bagged a pair! However, he slowly began to make a name for himself in the middle-order of the Essex batting line-up. I remember an innings of 94 at Old Trafford in the game against

Lancashire that included two sixes and 13 fours. His maiden first-class century came towards the end of that season, 114 not out against Leicestershire at Chelmsford; his powerful driving bringing victory to Essex off the last ball of the penultimate over.

He began the 1975 season in superb form. He hit 100 against Kent, 85 against Lancashire and 90 against Nottinghamshire and was selected for the MCC in their match against Australia at Lord's, hitting a sparkling 75. By the middle of the season, he had passed 700 runs and was awarded his county cap. This belligerent style also brought him a well-earned place in the England team for the first Test at Edgbaston, where he made a 'pair'. He played again at Lord's but didn't do enough for the selectors to consider him for the remainder of the series. The result was damaging to his confidence as his scores in the second half of that summer go to show.

He spent the next couple of seasons in rehabilitation, though he did rediscover his lost confidence to be chosen for England's one-day side in 1976.

In 1978, he began to open the innings for Essex and was a great success. In the early part of the season Essex beat both Kent and Northamptonshire by an innings. Against Kent, Gooch scored 108 and 129 against Northamptonshire, helping Ken McEwan add 321 to break the Essex second wicket record. He won back his England place and in the three Tests against New Zealand, he was England's leading batsman with an average of 63.33.

He toured Australia in 1978–79 and though he didn't have a particularly successful time with the bat (except for the last Test, where he hit a brilliant 74 on an indifferent wicket) his contribution to the tour in terms of fielding was outstanding. It was on this tour that Graham sought advice from the late Ken Barrington about his batting technique, resulting in the now familiar stance with the bat raised in readiness for the bowler's delivery.

When Essex won the County Championship in 1979, Gooch only played in 10 matches. Opening the batting allowed him more time to build an innings and give the county an attacking look right from the start. In the Benson and Hedges Cup quarter-final tie with Warwickshire at Chelmsford, Gooch treated the full-house to a display of awesome hitting in an innings of 138 (an enormous six and 19 fours). In the final against Surrey, he played a magnificent innings of 120 (three sixes and 11 fours) – it was the first of a run of successes in Lord's finals that Gooch was to maintain. He played in the four Tests against India (average 41.40) and in the World Cup.

In 1979–80 he was run out for 99 at Melbourne still seeking that elusive first Test century.

At the beginning of the 1980 season he hit the first double hundred of his career, 205 against Cambridge University. In the second Test at Lord's, he hit his maiden Test century against the West Indies, a magnificent 123 made out of the first 165 runs (he'd already made 1,000 runs in Test cricket prior to his first century).

In 1980–81, he toured the West Indies and was by far the most successful of the English batsmen, scoring 116 at Bridgetown and 153 at Kingston, to average 57.50 in the series. Playing only nine Championship matches for Essex in 1981, he was very successful, but in averaging only 13.90 for the first five Tests, he was dropped for the last Test in the six match series against Australia.

In 1981–82, he enjoyed personal success under the leadership of Keith Fletcher on England's trip to India, hitting a superb 127 in the fifth Test at Madras. In the fourth Test at Calcutta, he entertained the large crowd by bowling slow left-arm spin in the closing stages, imitating Dilip Doshi! He also showed his prowess at golf by hitting a hole in one at the Tollygunge Golf Club.

In 1982 in the Benson and Hedges Cup zonal match at Hove, Gooch hit the Sussex attack for 198 not out (five sixes and 22 fours) – it was the highest score made in a one-day competition in England. He also equalled the county record for five catches in an innings against Gloucestershire at Cheltenham College (six in the match to also equal the record). As well as a splendid mime of famous contemporary bowling actions, he had developed into a more than useful medium-pace swing bowler, producing his best figures of 7 for 14 against Worcestershire at Ilford.

In 1983, Gooch once again took the Cambridge University bowlers apart, hitting 174 in an opening stand of 263 with Brian Hardie. In the one-day game, Essex scored 310 for 5 against Glamorgan at Southend, Gooch scoring 176 (off 117 balls), both establishing new John Player League records. He also took 122 off the Kent attack in the second round of the Nat West Bank Trophy.

He'd also made a decision to lead a rebel tour to South Africa and a three year suspension kept him out of the national side until the 1985 home series with Australia. Whatever the rights and wrongs of that issue, there is no doubt it greatly helped Essex's cause. He had been acting captain when Keith Fletcher was out of action and in 1984 was named vice-captain. His batting in that 1984 season was absolutely brilliant. Leading the side against Hampshire at Southampton, he won the toss and batted first, hitting the second double century of his career, 220 (five sixes and 29 fours). Against Derbyshire at Chesterfield, he hit 227 (five sixes and 32 fours). He was the first man that season to reach 2,000 runs – scoring 2,559, the highest by an Essex player in a season.

In 1985, Gooch hit 171 off 155 balls in the John Player League against Nottinghamshire at Trent Bridge. he set up a record opening partnership of 239 in 38 overs, hitting three sixes and 18 fours in his innings. He also hit 202 in the Championship fixture at Trent Bridge. The men from Nottinghamshire must have hated the sight of Gooch that season, for he hit 91 against them at Lord's in the Nat West Final, as he and Hardie (110) put 202 on for the first wicket. He scored 487 runs (average 54.11) against Australia, with a top score of 196 in the final Test at the Oval, England winning by an innings and 94 runs. He had a successful benefit, realizing £153,906 and at the end of the season replaced Keith Fletcher as captain.

On England's ill-fated tour of the West Indies, he was the only batsman to come out of the tour with any credit, hitting four fifties in the five Test series.

Under his leadership in 1986, Essex won the County Championship for the third time in four years and the fourth time in eight years. Due to his international calls (114 v India and 183 v New Zealand, both at Lord's) he was to miss eleven matches. He resigned after two seasons, when the responsibility of leading his county side coincided with a loss of batting form.

In 1988 he hit his highest score in the Championship, 275 against Kent at Chelmsford. He was appointed England's fourth captain against the West Indies when Chris Cowdrey withdrew because of injury: scoring 459 runs (average 45.90) and hitting 146 in the first Test at Trent Bridge. He led England to their first win in 18 Tests against Sri Lanka and was appointed captain for the 1988–89 tour of India (after he had withdrawn from a playing contract with Western Province). The tour however, was cancelled when the Indian government refused to issue entry visas to Gooch and seven other 'black-listed' members of the squad. During that 1988 season, he played in two first-class matches on 30 August – fielding for Essex v Surrey at the Oval after batting for England v Sri Lanka at Lord's.

He was re-appointed captain of Essex in 1989, following the retirement of Keith Fletcher. It was a season in which he disappointed in the Tests against the all-winning Australians (183 runs at 20.33) asking to be left out of the fifth Test, but ended the season with the highest ever Sunday League average, 95.66.

In 1989–90 he led England in their successful if not winning series in the West Indies. Due to injury, he only played in two Tests, but averaged 42.66.

He was the leading scorer in the 1980s decade, scoring 21,174 runs in all first-class matches with 59 centuries and an average of 49.01.

One could write a book alone on Graham's achievements in the 1990 season. He topped the national first-class batting averages, scoring 2,746 runs in all matches at an average of 101.70, including 12 hundreds. His top score was 215 against Leicestershire, an innings containing 1 six and 28 fours. His 65 against the same county in the Refuge Assurance League made him the eigth batsman to reach 6,000 runs on Sundays.

At Test level, he hit 154 against New Zealand in the third Test to finish second to Michael Atherton in the averages with 61.20. Against India, he scored 752 runs at an average of 125.33, amazingly once again finishing second in the averages to Robin Smith, who averaged 180.50. In the opening Test, he hit 333 off 485 balls, the innings lasting 627 minutes and containing three sixes and 43 fours – for good measure, he hit 123 in the second innings!

His progress towards being the prolific and exciting player that both Essex and England adore has been gradual. He is a batsman able to look after himself against any bowler and is now probably the best opening batsman in the world; he has a very sound technique, allied with tremendous power and a willingness to carry the attack.

CHARLES GREEN

Born: 26 August 1846, Walthamstow
Died: 4 December 1916
Did not play first-class cricket for Essex

Born in Walthamstow on 26 August 1846, Charles Green was educated at a private school in Brighton before attending Uppingham. Learning the game at Uppingham, he was one of the first men who earned that school any cricket reputation. On leaving Uppingham, he went to Cambridge and played in the University XI from 1865 to 1868, captaining the side in his last year. Initially at Cambridge he was thought of as a fast opening bowler, but he began to concentrate more and more on his batting. During his time at Cambridge the Light Blues won two and lost two of their encounters with Oxford. In 1868, Cambridge won by 168 runs with Green top scoring in each innings with 44 and 59.

In 1866, whilst still at Cambridge, he won six events at the Walthamstow Rifle Club Sports – high jump, long jump, 100 yards, hurdles, kicking the football and throwing the cricket ball. He also showed his athletic prowess at Cambridge, winning the mile in a time of 5 mins 4 secs and the Inter-Varsity high jump competition.

He first played county cricket for Sussex in 1868, but for ten years or so after, was a regular member of the Middlesex side and one of the most exciting amateurs in the land.

In 1870 at Lord's whilst playing for the MCC and Ground against Yorkshire, he played a great innings of 51. He and W G

Grace (66) batted bravely on a wicket quite unfit for a first-class match. Both Emmett and Freeman made the ball fly about on the rough ground and it was remarkable that neither batsman suffered injury.

In 1871, playing for the Gentlemen against the Players at the Oval, he scored 57 not out: it was considered one of his best ever innings. He made his last 27 runs from just seven strokes, winning the game for his side with just three minutes to spare.

In 1882, he joined Essex and became captain the following year. However, it is not just on the field of play that he should be measured. He took the County Club into a new age, persuading H H Stephenson to become coach at Uppingham and C D Buxton to remain with the county – he'd already persuaded A P 'Bunny' Lucas to come to Essex.

In 1883, his first year as captain, he led by example, scoring 235 runs at an average of 25.50. A year later, he and F H Stevens added 129 for the sixth wicket against Northamptonshire at Wellingborough; it was the first large stand for the new county club.

It was Charles Green who decided that a move away from Brentwood would be in the best interests of the County Club. He showed great vision in pushing for the ground at Leyton.

A most determined man, eager to put the Club on a professional basis, he gave way to Lucas as captain in 1888. However, he was still Chairman of the Club and played a prominent part in directing the county through the troubles that lay ahead. Along with Borradaile, it was Green who was to save the Club from extinction over the next few years.

The Father of Essex cricket, he was bitterly disappointed by the trend towards the importation of overseas players and the lack of support afforded to the County. He resigned as Chairman though he accepted the position of President. He played no further part in the running of the club, his last act being typical of the man, paying off the Club's debts of £400 so the new regime could start with a clean sheet.

A director of the Orient Steamship Company, he was President of the MCC in 1905.

As Master of the Essex Hunt for a long time, he became even more devoted to the sport of hunting than cricket, being out four days a week every season for many years.

His contribution to Essex County Cricket Club is immeasurable: without Charles Ernest Green, there would have been no County Club.

BILL GREENSMITH

Born: 16 August 1930, Middlesborough
Played: 1947–1963

FIRST-CLASS ESSEX RECORDS

Matches	Innings	NO	Runs	HS	Ave	100s
371	550	148	8,042	138*	20.05	1

Runs	Wkts	Ave	BB	5wI	10wm	Ct
20,711	720	28.76	8/59	21	2	147

TEST MATCHES – 0

Though he made his first-class debut in 1947 against Gloucestershire, it was some four years later, before Bill Greensmith, a young Yorkshire-born leg-spin bowler from Buckhurst Hill, fulfilled his early promise. In that 1951 season, he took 46 wickets in the County Championship.

In 1952 against Leicestershire he showed real potential as an all-rounder. Batting at number 10, he hit a quick-fire 79 before destroying the Midlands side by taking 6 for 44 in their second innings. In fact, the first five wickets of this spell were taken in 31 balls without a single run being taken off him – Essex winning the game by 107 runs. He'd started the season well, but as it wore on, he became a little expensive, though he did take 20 catches in the field.

In 1953, Bill Greensmith hit his maiden first-class century, 138 not out. In 1955, he had a very satisfying season, scoring 698 runs at an average of 23.26 and picking up 84 wickets at 26.42 runs each. Greensmith's leg-breaks and googlies caused problems for many top batsmen.

In 1956, he enjoyed yet another good season as an all-rounder, taking 80 wickets at 21.07 each and scoring 544 runs. In 1957 Greensmith bowled well, his leg-spinners claiming 63 victims, this in spite of him missing several matches through injury.

After a disappointing summer the following year, in which he was left out of the side, Greensmith bounced back in 1959 and turned in some creditable performances, including 6 for 40 in the 21 run win against Sussex at Brentwood.

In 1960, his batting outshone his bowling, as he met with far greater success than many recognised batsmen.

In 1961, he took 64 wickets at a cost of 26.15 runs apiece. He took 4 for 18 in Derbyshire's second innings, as they collapsed to 137 all out, enabling Essex to win by 181 runs after trailing by 60 runs on the first innings.

In 1962, Greensmith had another useful season, hitting 764 runs and collecting 77 wickets. His best performance with the ball came in the match against Lancashire at Liverpool, when he took 7 for 59, Essex winning by 28 runs.

In his testimonial year, 1963, Greensmith suffered the fate of so many Essex beneficiaries and lost his place in the side early in the season through ill-health. When he did reappear, his bowling form had completely deserted him and he announced his retirement at the end of the season.

Bill Greensmith was a more than useful bat and leg-spinner who turned in consistent performances for the county in a 17 year spell.

BRIAN HARDIE

Born: 14 January 1950, Stenhousemuir
Played: 1973–1990

FIRST-CLASS ESSEX RECORDS

Matches	Innings	NO	Runs	HS	Ave	100s
367	590	76	17,466	162	33.98	26

Runs	Wkts	Ave	BB	5wI	10wm	Ct
254	3	84.66	2/39	–	–	331

TEST MATCHES – 0

Brian Ross Hardie was born in Stenhousemuir, Stirlingshire on 14 January 1950. He was educated at Larbert High School and it wasn't long before he was playing for his home town team in the East of Scotland League. Like his father and brother Keith, he went on to play for Scotland, making his debut in 1970. The following year he scored a century in each innings in the match against the MCC at Aberdeen, but as the match wasn't regarded as first-class the performance wasn't recognized. However, it had certainly been noted and he joined Essex before the start of the 1973 season.

During the following season he became a regular opening batsman. He came into the public eye after hitting just four runs in 142 minutes against Hampshire at Chelmsford – the Essex record for the slowest innings! He hit his maiden first-class century at Ilford against Middlesex; it took him five hours, gaining him a reputation as a slow dour Scottish batsman – how wrong they were. Also that season he hit 133 against Warwickshire, as Essex won by an innings. He once again topped 1,000 runs in 1975, making the highest score of his career, 162 against Warwickshire at Edgbaston, but struggled the following season, only scoring 372 runs in County Championship matches.

After a couple of poor seasons, Hardie moved to the middle-order and Gooch became opener. He showed a great determination in an effort to overcome his technical limitations. Few who saw him in those early years would have put money on his making runs at county level for 18 seasons. He later reverted to opener, but it didn't matter where Brian Hardie batted, he was a batsman for all occasions and all positions.

During 1979 he hit his first century at Ilford in the match against Lancashire, Essex winning by an innings. He produced a fighting innings with an unbeaten century against Hampshire at Bournemouth as Essex won again by an innings. When Essex clinched the County Championship at Northampton, Hardie hit a century to see his side to victory by 7 wickets, after they'd been 25 runs behind on the first innings. He was an outstanding fielder at short-leg, picking up 30 catches in both 1979 and 1983.

The season of 1979 saw him produce his best bowling performance when he took 2 for 39 against Glamorgan at Ilford. In 1980–81 he began the first of two seasons playing in New Zealand club cricket, also playing for Auckland in 1988–89.

In 1981 he hit 108 not out against Yorkshire at Chelmsford in a John Player League match, helping Graham Gooch put on 180 in 30 overs for the first wicket. He began the 1983 season with a bang, hitting 129 against Cambridge University as he and Graham Gooch put on 263 for the first wicket – a fitting start to his benefit year.

In the match against Somerset at Southend in 1985, Hardie equalled his highest score with 162. He hit 110 in Essex's first Championship win in 1986 against Yorkshire, returning after having a broken hand to play a fine innings. He also scored 113 not out in the match against Somerset as Essex won an improbable victory by 9 runs. Essex retained the John Player League trophy, perhaps the most important win coming against Nottinghamshire at Trent Bridge. In this match, Hardie and Gooch set up a new John Player League record opening partnership with a stand of 239 in 38 overs. They continued with other one-day opening stands of note with 139 in 27.3 overs against Sussex in the Benson and Hedges Cup and 184 in 28 overs against Warwickshire in the John Player League. Hardie also hit 113 against the Combined Universities at Chelmsford in the Benson and Hedges Cup.

Probably his greatest moment came in the 1985 Nat West Trophy Final win over Nottinghamshire. Hardie and Gooch put on 202 for the first wicket; it was the highest partnership in any Lord's Final, with Hardie's score being 110. He reached his century in the 44th over off 136 deliveries and had hit 14 fours. It was his first century in the 60-over competition and was a brilliant piece of batting – deservedly winning him the Man of the Match award.

In 1986 he hit two further one-day hundreds that were his highest scores in the respective competitions; 109 in the John Player League against Northamptonshire at Colchester and 119 not out against Sussex in a Benson and Hedges Cup match at Hove.

'Lager', his long-time nickname, decided to retire at the end of the 1990 season, making his announcement while riding high in the national batting averages. His departure now leaves captain Graham Gooch as the only survivor of the regular Essex side of 1979 which won the County Championship.

He hit two centuries last summer to finish thrid in the Essex batting averages with 72.80.

A player with a great sense of humour, he was the most reliable of county cricketers – unorthodox with the disconcerting habit of hitting the ball in improbable directions – he will be missed.

AUGUSTUS HIPKIN

Born: 8 August 1900, Brancaster
Died: 11 February 1957
Played: 1923–1931

FIRST-CLASS EXSSEX RECORDS

Matches	Innings	NO	Runs	HS	Ave	100s
231	326	55	4,239	108	15.64	2

Runs	Wkts	Ave	BB	5wI	10wm	Ct
13,377	518	25.82	8/71	18	3	209

TEST MATCHES – 0

Augustus Bernard Hipkin or 'Joe' as he was more commonly known, was a discovery of Johnnie Douglas. Born in Brancaster, Norfolk, he arrived at Essex from the Loughton Club.

He made his debut in 1923, taking 49 wickets. He was a slow left-arm bowler who spun the ball a great deal and who could flight it cleverly. It has been said that Johnnie Douglas spoiled Hipkin by bullying him, though most people believed it was Hipkin himself who was his own worst enemy, because despite his obvious talent, he didn't possess the temperament to be a really top-flight spinner.

Perhaps the match between Essex and Middlesex at Leyton in 1923 best sums up the Hipkin – Douglas relationship. Middlesex had scored 489 and Essex were standing at 137 for 6. Douglas and Morris made a stand and then Franklin (who hit his maiden century) joined Douglas for a ninth wicket stand of 160 in just over two hours. Middlesex were already using their twelfth man, when another injury caused the need for them to borrow Essex's twelfth man, who happened to be Augustus Hipkin. Douglas was on 96 when he hit a delivery towards the leg boundary. Hipkin running at full stretch took a brilliant one-handed catch. Hipkin went round to the amateurs' dressing room to apologise to Douglas – his reply 'You bloody fool, Hipkin. I would have broken your neck if you had missed it'.

By 1924, Hipkin had made a great advance as a spin bowler and took 116 wickets at a cost of 21.72 runs apiece. He topped the county's bowling averages; his best figures being 8 for 71 against Gloucestershire at Bristol. Hipkin also performed the hat-trick against Lancashire at Blackpool, his victims being Len Hopwood, Dick Tyldesley and George Duckworth, the England wicket-keeper.

In 1925 he began to show signs of developing into an all-rounder, scoring 620 runs and taking the most wickets, 81 at a cost of 21.29 runs each. He also developed a reputation as a good fieldsman, taking 30 catches in the 1926 season.

The following season saw him score over 900 runs, including two centuries, his highest score being 108. There were times during his first-class career, when his batting performances almost equalled his ability as a bowler and fieldsman.

Hipkin was a gifted sportsman, being a professional footballer, playing as a goalkeeper – this undoubtedly aided his fielding, and he took 34 catches in both 1927 and 1929.

In his last season, 1931, he only took 4 wickets and at the end of the summer Essex decided not to renew his contract. He went to Scotland, meeting with great success as professional with the Uddingstone and West of Scotland clubs.

In all first-class matches, he took 528 wickets at a cost of 25.56 runs, accumulated 4,446 runs at an average of 16.40 and fielded with great ability.

He died in a Lanarkshire hospital on 11 February 1957 at the age of 56.

ROBIN HOBBS

Born: 8 May 1942 , Chippenham
Played: 1961–1975

FIRST-CLASS ESSEX RECORDS

Matches	Innings	NO	Runs	HS	Ave	100s
325	429	102	4,069	100	12.44	2

Runs	Wkts	Ave	BB	5wl	10wm	Ct
19,844	763	26.00	8/63	32	5	222

TEST MATCHES – 7

Born in Chippenham in 1942 while his father was still in the RAF, Robin left Wiltshire when only a few weeks old and spent several years in Scotland before settling in Essex., At school, he was a natural ball player, an outstanding wing three-quarter for Raines Grammar School and a quick leg-break bowler, who could demolish most young sides lacking in experience against his type of bowling.

By the age of 15, he was playing for Chadwell Heath and had represented the Employers Liability Insurance Company before his sixteenth birthday. Against another insurance company he scored a century which gained him a new bat and a meeting with the great Jack Hobbs in his Fleet Street sports shop. This type of performance suggested to his employers that he was a better cricketer than insurance clerk and they offered no protest when Robin decided to make a career in cricket.

Although recognized as an Essex player, it was a rather belated decision by the county to secure his services for they were well staffed with spinners. Kent offered him terms, but Trevor Bailey, then the Essex secretary and captain, refused to release him and so he joined the Essex staff in 1960 as the ninth spinner!

In his first year, he played only half a dozen matches for the 2nd XI and it wasn't until 1961 that he made his first-class debut. It came against Leicestershire at Ilford. There was a seamers' wicket and he did not bowl. It was against Gloucestershire at Stroud that he took his first four wickets in county cricket. By the end of his first season, he had taken 23 wickets at a cost of 28.65 runs apiece.

After appearing in county games since the age of 19 he was asked to go on a Cavaliers tour to Jamaica in the winter of 1962–63: he played in all four matches and bowled well.

59

In 1964, Hobbs took 81 wickets with his leg-breaks and was chosen to tour South Africa with the MCC in the coming winter months. Also this season, he showed his value as a quick run-getter. In the match against Hampshire at Southampton, Essex were required to score 201 in 138 minutes. Essex enjoyed this type of challenge and won by five wickets with eight minutes to spare. Robin Hobbs taking 19 off four successive Derek Shackleton deliveries – 6,6,4,3.

In 1965 Hobbs took 75 wickets at a cost of 23.36 runs each. He took 5 for 46 against Worcestershire and had match figures of 12 for 94 in the match against Glamorgan at Llanelli.

In 1966 he took 88 wickets in all matches at 25.77 runs each. When Essex entertained Somerset at Ilford (the first county match to include Sunday play) there was a close finish. Essex were on 284 for 7 and Hobbs needed to hit the last ball of the match for six, unfortunately he only got two and the match was drawn – however, he was probably the right man for the job. In the drawn game with Glamorgan he bowled exceptionally well to claim match figures of 13 for 164, including his career best bowling figures in the Welsh side's first innings, 8 for 63.

Robin Hobbs was one of the last regular leg-spinners in the country and a most brilliant of fielders. He made some useful contributions with the bat and made seven appearances for his country. His first England appearance came in 1967 in the series against India, Hobbs producing his best international figures, 3 for 25 at Edgbaston. He took 12 wickets in his seven appearances for his country.

In 1968 Essex were 185 for 7 against Glamorgan when Robin Hobbs joined Stuart Turner. Between them, they hit 192 in just two hours – Hobbs hit his maiden century and went on to take seven wickets.

He wasn't used as much as he should have been in the one-day game, considering that in 1968 he took a hat-trick against Middlesex at Lord's in the Gillette Cup, his victims being R W Hooker, J S E Price and R S Herman. The following season, Essex beat the New Zealanders by 15 runs at Westcliff, Hobbs taking 6 for 88 in the match. During the winter of 1969–70, he toured the Caribbean as a member of the Duke of Norfolk's side. He was by far the most successful bowler. In 1970 he had a fine season, floating his leg-spinners higher and higher for greater reward. He took 90 wickets for Essex and topped the bowling averages, but in all the matches, he took 102 wickets at 21.40 runs each. In 1973 he took 6 for 22 against Hampshire at Harlow in the John Player League, just another example of his one-day form.

Hobbs's benefit year was in 1974 and this, coupled with leading the side in Fletcher's absence, did not help his form.

In 1975 he scored 100 in 44 minutes against the Australians at

Chelmsford. It was the fastest hundred for 55 years. He hit seven sixes and 12 fours and his second fifty took only 12 minutes. At the time, it was the fifth fastest ever recorded in first-class cricket. It was most certainly the fastest by any Essex player and the fastest conceded by any touring team. His longest hit landed on the river bank about 90 yards away. However, Essex lost the match by 98 runs and Hobbs was, rather surprisingly, left out of the Essex side for the next match at Northampton.

Robin Hobbs wasn't a big spinner of the ball, but extremely accurate for his style, varying the flight and pace skilfully. He used to bowl off a six pace approach and would be momentarily off the ground, his arms stretched wide and his body slightly twisting as he put everything into the wrist spin to make the ball go through quickly.

He retired prematurely to pursue a career in commerce and play for Suffolk. He had another year of his contract with Essex to run and could have had another after that if he had wanted it.

He later joined Glamorgan as captain (not surprising when one considers his performances with both bat and ball against them) in 1979, playing until the end of the 1981 season.

Hobbs was disappointed that the paying public seemed only to be interested in the number of fours and sixes being hit and not the subtleties of his bowling, which most certainly was an art in itself.

DOUG INSOLE

Born: 18 April 1926, Clapton, Middlesex
Played: 1947–1963
Averages in all first-class Essex matches

FIRST-CLASS ESSEX RECORDS

Matches	Innings	NO	Runs	HS	Ave	100s	
345	574	54	20,113	219*	38.67	48	

Runs	Wkts	Ave	BB	5wl	10wm	Ct	St
4,061	119	34.12	5/22	1	–	279	1

TEST MATCHES – 9

Doug Insole, like Trevor Bailey played his early cricket whilst at Cambridge University. In 1947 after the university term, he appeared for Essex in their remaining games, hitting his first century for the county, 109 not out against Lancashire at Clacton. At the end of the summer he had scored 1,237 runs.

In 1949, after captaining Cambridge, he returned to Essex, where he topped the batting averages with 850 championship runs at an average of 65.38. In that season, he hit a superb unbeaten 219 against Yorkshire in a drawn game at Castle Park, Colchester.

In 1950, Insole was appointed joint-captain with Tom Pearce; the step was taken initially to give Insole the benefit of Pearce's experience before he took over as captain the following season but in fact he assumed the captaincy in June of that year. Insole had a successful season in 1950, scoring 1,981 runs at an average of 34.73 with four hundreds. He also made his England debut this summer, appearing in the third Test against the West Indies at Trent Bridge. Insole also hit 106 for Essex against Warwickshire in what was the first televised County Championship match.

In 1951 Doug Insole's appointment as first-team captain was confirmed. His approach to the game as captain was very professional and more realistic than his predecessor, Tom Pearce. He brought to the job a burning enthusiasm, shrewdness and imagination. He was a great believer in the art of fielding and, during his reign, he raised the standard of Essex fielding. He finished top of the Essex batting averages in that first season as captain, scoring 2,032 runs in all matches at an average of 42.33. He was also chosen for the Gentlemen v Players match at Lord's, scoring 50 and 44 not out.

Insole scored 1,816 runs in 1952 and passed the landmark again the following season, hitting a magnificent 116 against the touring Indians.

In 1954 he scored 1,841 runs in all matches, heading the Essex batting averages. In the match against Northamptonshire at Romford, he came close to registering a century in each innings. He scored a superb unbeaten 156 in the first innings and, as captain, he declared the Essex second innings with his own score on 92 not out.

Doug Insole had the best season of his career in 1955, scoring 2,427 runs; more than anyone else in the country and including nine hundreds. He scored two of them, 111 and 118 in the same match against Kent at Gillingham and two off the white-rose attack, 142 at Bradford and 119 at Southend. He hit 114 not out against Nottinghamshire at Southend: his hundred, like that of his partner Bailey, coming up before lunch. He hit 129 against the South Africans at Colchester and was selected for the fourth Test at Headingley. He also captained the Gentlemen against the Players at Lord's and was chosen as one of Wisden's 'Five Cricketers of the Year'.

Insole had gained his Blue for football and appeared for Corinthian Casuals in the 1955–56 F.A. Amateur Cup Final at Wembley against Bishop Auckland.

In 1956, Insole was once again in tremendous form, scoring 1,988 runs in all matches at an average of 41.41. He hit four hundreds and was the first batsman in the country to reach 1,000 runs. Yet again he made just one Test appearance that summer against the Australians at Headingley but was part of the side to tour South Africa, going as Peter May's vice-captain.

The following season, he scored 1,725 runs in all matches. His best innings was probably the 115 in the second innings of the match against Surrey at Clacton, which steered his side to victory. He was chosen also for his one customary Test match. All this came after he'd returned from South Africa topping the English Test match batting averages. He represented his country on nine occasions, his top score of 110 not out coming at Durban in the third Test of that 1956–57 tour.

In 1958, Insole suffered an injury batting against Somerset at Ilford; although it took him some time to recover fully, he still surpassed the 1,000 run mark scoring 1,220 runs at an average of 30.50. His best performance came in the match with Sussex at Hove, Insole scoring 108 and 51.

By 1959, he was back to his brilliant best, scoring 2,045 runs in all matches at an average of 45.44. In Ken Preston's benefit match against Gloucestershire at Leyton, he hit 177 not out and 90, driving and pulling magnificently. There were 25 fours and 2 sixes in his unbeaten 177 – made in only 3½ hours. The match was tied, Gloucestershire failing by one run to make 212. During the season Insole was appointed a Test selector, this meaning that he played in fewer matches for Essex. His selectorial duties the following summer didn't stop him from reaching the 1,000 run mark, scoring 1,269 in all matches, including three centuries. One of these was against the South Africans at Ilford, but Essex still lost by six wickets.

At the end of the 1960 season, after leading Essex to sixth place in the championship, Insole announced his decision to resign from the position of captain, to concentrate upon his business career.

As a captain, Insole led from the front; he believed in playing attractive cricket, his Essex side twice winning the News Chronicle 'Brighter Cricket Table'. He was always willing to issue or accept a challenge. He made a large number of runs for Essex. Every year he was among the leading batsmen and at his best against off-spin, inswing and in a crisis.

On his retirement from the first-class game at the end of the 1963 season, he continued to give great service to the game of cricket, both to Essex and the sport in general. He has been a Test selector, chairman of the TCCB and an MCC Committee member and the manager of two tours to Australia.

He was also one of England's two negotiators at the 1989 ICC special meeting which agreed a ban on players visiting South Africa.

An unconventional batsman with a wonderful eye in his playing days, he was awarded the CBE for his services to the game and at the time of writing is chairman of Essex County Cricket Club.

BARRY KNIGHT

Born: 18 February 1938, Chesterfield
Played: 1955–1966

FIRST-CLASS ESSEX RECORDS

Matches	Innings	NO	Runs	HS	Ave	100s
239	399	42	8,798	165	24.64	8

Runs	Wkts	Avge	BB	5wI	10wm	Ct
17,162	761	22.55	8/69	39	8	171

TEST MATCHES – 29

Before he was ten years old, Barry Knight showed an ability with both bat and ball and was under instruction from Harry Lee, the former Middlesex opening bat, who was coaching at the indoor school in Chiswick. Harry Sharp also helped during Knight's formative years and developed his natural talent until he joined the Essex coaching school. He had played representative cricket for East Ham Grammar School, London Schools and South of England Schools and, at the age of 16, was invited to a pre-season 1st XI practice at Chelmsford. He was so impressive with the bat that Trevor Bailey offered him a contract without seeing him bowl!

Essex called on him for the county side when he was only 17 but the gap between school cricket and the first-class game was too much for him, so after a couple of matches he joined the RAF for National Service. During this period he played a few games for the county, but one of these included the match against the West Indies, where Collie Smith and Frank Worrell took 17 off one of his overs, which included four no-balls. Not surprisingly, he was not asked to reappear again until his service career was completed.

By 1959 he had made a tremendous leap forward as an all-rounder. He just missed the 'double' by five runs, scoring 995 at an average of 27.63 and capturing 101 wickets at 23.56 runs each. He hit his maiden century 103 against Worcestershire at Leyton, driving stylishly following on the game at Westcliff against Kent, where he'd taken 10 wickets in the match (5 for 83 and 5 for 63). He topped the county bowling averages and, not surprisingly, was awarded his county cap. He made a good impression too in the match against the Indians scoring 89.

An injury late in the 1960 season kept Knight out for several matches, but his bowling was of such a high quality, that he still captured 88 wickets. He revelled in the Westcliff wickets, taking 6 for 88 and 7 for 55 against Glamorgan and 5 wickets in the Middlesex match, which was curtailed by rain. Also at Headingley against Yorkshire, he took 6 for 45 in the match as Yorkshire were bowled out for 86.

In 1961, the 'double' still eluded him, with 1,148 runs at 25.51 and taking 89 wickets at a cost of 23.95 runs apiece. In the match at Westcliff, Essex beat Nottinghamshire by 120 runs, Knight scoring 912 and capturing 7 wickets., Against Somerset, also in the Westcliff week, Knight scored a quick-fire 34 and took 6 for 23 as Somerset were shot out for 48, Essex winning by 106 runs. In the next match, he pulled a stomach-muscle and this hampered his performances for some time.

In 1962, Barry Knight achieved his first 'double', scoring 1,689 runs at an average of 34.46 and capturing 100 wickets at 24.05 runs apiece. Along with R.A.G. Luckin he put on 206 against Middlesex to equal the 1923 Essex 6th wicket record. His form was so good that against Pakistan at Trent Bridge he took 4 for 38 (his best bowling figures for England). At the end of the season he was chosen to tour Australia with the MCC side. Essex also defeated Pakistan, Knight taking 4 for 66. This summer also saw Knight play an innings of 88 against Warwickshire at Edgbaston, all but four of his runs coming in boundaries.

During the 1962–63 close season, he clinched one Test victory for England against New Zealand at Christchurch, by hitting successive deliveries for 6, 4 and 4. In the first Test at Auckland, he and Peter Parfitt put on 240 for the 6th wicket – still an English record in all Tests.

In 1963, Knight had an excellent season, performing the 'double' for the second consecutive season. He scored 1,578 runs at an average of 28.69 and took 140 wickets at 21.72 runs each. There were nine occasions during the summer that he took five or more wickets in an innings. He wasn't chosen for any of the Test matches against the West Indies, in spite of bowling figures of 8 for 69 against Nottinghamshire at Trent Bridge, 8 for 70 against Gloucestershire at Gloucester and 7 for 68 against Middlesex at

Southend. However, he was chosen for the MCC tour of India in 1963–64. Against Hampshire at Ilford, Knight had a good all-round game, scoring 124 and taking 4 for 39 in Hampshire's first innings. I have mentioned his 8 for 69 in the match against Nottinghamshire, but in the same game, he scored 58 and 101 not out to clinch a 57 run win for Essex.

In 1964, Knight scored 1,209 runs at an average of 23.25 and took 100 wickets at a cost of 27.02 runs each. At the end of the season Knight won the Carling single-wicket competition, beating the popular Northamptonshire opener Colin Milburn in the final at Lord's.

The following season, despite it being a wet one, Knight yet again performed the 'double'. He scored 1,172 runs (average 22.98) and took 125 wickets at 18.90 runs. In fact, he was the only first-class cricketer that summer to achieve the feat. This he did on a sultry August Bank Holiday afternoon, driving a ball from Middlesex's Ron Hooker through the covers on the Leyton ground for four. He topped the Essex bowling averages and almost bowled Essex to a win against Yorkshire at Bradford, taking 5 for 41 and 5 for 49 as Yorkshire hung on in their second innings at 198 for 9, needing 199 to avoid an innings defeat. He took 6 for 30 against Middlesex at Leyton, Essex winning by 9 wickets. At the end of the season he was presented by the Essex Committee with a cheque for 100 guineas and a clock in recognition of his being the only cricketer to perform the 'double'.

In 1966 he was chosen for the second Test match at Lord's against the West Indies, but his form had slipped somewhat. He scored 776 runs (average 19.89) and took 83 wickets at 21.16 runs apiece.

Knight was a very good all-round cricketer. As a batsman, he was a superb player of slow bowling, occasionally struggling against real pace. As a bowler, he could generate quite an amount of pace himself and was often lethal when aided by the pitch. He originally bowled mainly inswingers at a very lively pace, but became a much better bowler when he cut down and learned how to take the ball away from the bat off the seam. At Chalkwell Park in Westcliff, Knight had a strong affection for the 'green' track and could usually be relied upon to take 20 wickets during the week.

Following the appointment of Brian Taylor as captain at the end of the 1966 season, Knight decided to leave the Club and joined Leicestershire mid-way through the 1968 season.

On leaving the first-class game in England he emigrated to Australia continuing to play a high-standard of grade cricket with the Mosman Club in Sydney. Cricket is still the centre of his life, as he now manages a successful cricket school.

A highly talented all-rounder, Knight made a massive contribution to Essex cricket.

CHARLES KORTRIGHT

Born: 9 January 1871, Ingatestone
Died: 12 December 1952
Played: 1894–1907

FIRST-CLASS ESSEX RECORDS

Matches	Innings	NO	Runs	HS	Ave	100s
160	255	18	4,182	131	17.64	2

Runs	Wkts	Ave	BB	5wI	10wm	Ct
9,036	440	20.53	8/57	35	8	167

TEST MATCHES – 0

Charles Jesse Kortright was born at Ingatestone on 9 January 1871 and educated at Brentwood and Tonbridge Schools. He left Tonbridge with a reputation of being 'a very fast bowler with a high puzzling delivery and often very difficult to play. Ought to develop into a first class bowler.'

Kortright joined the Brentwood Club and was soon a success. He took 89 wickets at 6 runs apiece in 1889 at just eighteen years of age. His performances soon attracted Essex and he was invited to play against Leicestershire at Leyton. He was only allowed to bowl two overs at the close of the match and took the wicket of Mr H T Arnall – Thompson. He then moved to Hythe in Kent to learn the brewery trade. He played a lot of club cricket in Kent and resisted the offer to play for the hop county. He was considered to be the fastest bowler of all time by many.

In 1891 Kortright and Pickett put on 244 for the eighth wicket in the game against Hampshire at Southampton. Essex won by an innings, Kortright hitting 158 in one-and-threequarter hours, including four sixes, a five and 22 fours. It was the highest individual score recorded for Essex at that time. On the bowling front, he took 36 wickets at a cost of 11.80 runs each. He took 8 wickets in an innings on three occasions, against Derbyshire, Hampshire and the MCC, all at Leyton. Whilst playing for Hythe and still learning the brewery trade, he took five School of Musketry wickets in five balls.

He took 8 for 29 and 5 for 35 in 1893 as Surrey were dismissed for 54 and 76 respectively in the fixture at Leyton. He took 8 Yorkshire wickets in the match at Sheffield, Essex winning by seven wickets inside two days. Kortright was, without doubt, one of the season's great successes. He was described as 'fast, very fast' and had been elected a member of the MCC at the beginning of the season, so that he could be considered for the match against the Australians. He was also selected for the Gentlemen against the Players at Lord's. It was his highest honour outside the Test match arena. The match was drawn, but he took 7 for 73 and 2 for 67. There are reports that on dismissing Lancashire's John Briggs in the first innings, he sent a stump reeling back some 17 yards! William Gunn, the famous Nottinghamshire batsman, said after Kortright had beaten him in this fixture that the ball which did it was a yard faster than any he had ever played against.

In 1895, Kortright took 8 for 94, as Warwickshire were dismissed for 259 in a drawn game. Though Essex were beaten by Leicestershire by 75 runs that summer, Kortright took 8 for 63 in their second innings. He took 7 for 57 as Somerset were bowled out for 129. Against Derbyshire he had match figures of 13 for 103. By 1895 he had raised enough capital from his share in the Hythe Brewery to enjoy the life of a gentleman cricketer for the rest of his career. When Essex entertained Surrey at Leyton, Kortright had figures of 7 for 72, including the wickets of Hayward, Druce, Abel, Lohmann, Read and Street in the space of 15 balls for just 4 runs. Despite this, Surrey still won by 201 runs!

In 1896 Essex dismissed the MCC at Lord's for just 41, Kortright taking 6 for 23 (10 for 57 in the match) as Essex won by an innings. In the match against Yorkshire at Huddersfield, Kortright destroyed the white-rose middle-order with some ferocious bowling. He was barracked by the crowd after striking Yorkshire batsman Moorhouse with a rising delivery. Kortright was fast but fair, yet he had the temperament of a great fast bowler. Home Gordon wrote in 1939, that Kortright was the fastest bowler he ever saw and one that was willing to hurt the batsman.

He had a good season in 1897, though he was never chosen for England. International selection was much more limited in his day. He took 11 wickets in the match against Leicestershire as the midlands county were beaten by 6 wickets. Ranjitsinhji saved the game for Sussex after Kortright had hit a blistering 74 and taken 5 wickets.

In 1898 Kortright bowled splendidly to take 12 for 106 against Lancashire as Essex won by 9 wickets in this match at Leyton. This was also the season that Kortright hit the first of his two first-class hundreds, 112 against Leicestershire. He backed this up with 6 for 41, Essex winning by an innings. In the match against Hampshire, he was in inspired form, taking 6 for 10 in the space of ten minutes, as Essex won with just fifteen minutes remaining. This season also saw Essex's first confrontation with Gloucestershire at Leyton and a meeting with W G Grace. Essex were dismissed for 128, with W G taking 7 for 44. Gloucestershire totalled 231,

Kortright taking 5 for 41, Grace hitting a masterly 126. Essex rallied somewhat in their second innings and reached 250. This left Gloucestershire requiring 148 to win but Kortright, bowling at his fiercest, dismissed both openers without a run on the board. Essex thought they'd got the breakthrough when Grace was caught off Mead, but refused to walk, thinking it was a bump ball and umpire Burton retracted his decision. Kortright believed the great man guilty of gamesmanship and delivered a spell of sustained short pitched bowling to Grace. It left him battered and blue, but not out and Gloucestershire finished the day on 81 for 3. The last morning saw Kortright appeal for lbw when Grace was on 49, then Grace edged the next delivery into the hands of wicket-keeper Russell, only to be given not out. Finally, he uprooted Grace's middle stump and as the Doctor was leaving, it is reputed Kortright uttered 'Surely you're not going Doctor, there's still one stump standing.' Kortright finished with 7 for 57 in the innings (12 for 98 in the match) but Gloucestershire won with the last pair at the wicket.

Kortright used to run in 15 yards, delivering the ball from his full height of six feet. He was both very fast and very straight. Between the years 1895 and 1898, he took 287 wickets for Essex, 206 of them were without any assistance from his fielders.

After straining his back in an accident at home he missed the entire 1899 season and was never quite the same again. He returned to the side in 1900 and began in great style by taking ten wickets in the victory over Gloucestershire. In the following match against Surrey at the Oval, he took 5 for 39 as the home side were dismissed for 78 as they chased 84 to win. In between the Surrey match and a victory over Leicestershire by an innings (when Kortright took 7 wickets in their second innings) was a defeat by Kent at Maidstone. He also took 8 for 57 against Yorkshire at Leyton and finished with 61 wickets in what proved to be his last really effective season as a fast bowler.

In 1903 Charles Kortright was invited to captain Essex. It was something of a strange choice. Kortright was now primarily a batsman, occasionally bowling a few overs of leg-spin and pace. It was a mixed season for the county under his leadership, Essex winning 7 and losing 6 of their 20 matches. For Kortright himself, he averaged only 12 with the bat and took 28 wickets at 14.21 runs each from 118.2 overs. After one year in office, he surprised the Essex AGM by announcing that he was standing down as skipper.

He played his last game for Essex against Middlesex at Leyton in 1907. He took 1 for 20 in Middlesex's second innings, his final victim being Pelham Warner.

In 1911 he was asked to consider coming out of retirement to take over as captain again. He was now 40 years of age, but despite taking a month to think things over, he rejected it.

Kortright was fond of recounting great tales. He told of a club match at Wallingford, where, so he declared, he bowled a ball which rose almost straight and went out of the ground without a second bounce – thus making him the first man to bowl six byes! He also claimed to have dismissed Brockwell of Surrey with a yorker which rebounded from the base of the stumps and went back past Kortright almost to the boundary.

Charles Kortright most surely was the fastest bowler the game has ever known. Why he never played for his country remains a mystery.

JOHN LEVER

Born: 24 February 1949, Stepney
Played: 1967–1989

FIRST-CLASS ESSEX RECORDS

Matches	Innings	NO	Runs	HS	Ave	100s
439	443	168	2,830	91	10.29	–

Runs	Wkts	Ave	BB	5wl	10wm	Ct
34,348	1,462	23.49	8/37	77	11	157

TEST MATCHES – 21

J K Lever was born in Stepney on 24 February 1949, making his Essex debut at the age of 18 in 1967. In his early days he showed plenty of promise as a batsman, hitting 91 against Glamorgan at Cardiff, after being sent in as nightwatchman. It has been said many times that, with a little more application to his batting, he could have become another Trevor Bailey. It was in the 1970 season, that he was awarded his county cap.

He was a captain's dream as a bowler: whatever the conditions or the state of the game, John Lever wanted to bowl. He was a very fit player, being able to keep going for long spells. As a fast-medium left-hander, his pace was sharp rather than genuinely quick. he had a long, relaxed run-up, a beautiful body action and a perfect follow-through. He had a superb command of line and length, which was why he had such a splendid record in limited overs cricket.

In 1972, in the Gillette Cup second round, he took 5 for 8 against Middlesex at Westcliff, as they were bowled out for 41. He also took 5 for 18 against Warwickshire at Edgbaston in a John Player League match. Three years later, he took 5 for 13 at Ebbw Vale against Glamorgan in a John Player match and in 1976, 5 for 16 against Middlesex at Chelmsford in the Benson and Hedges Cup. He continued to impress and certainly, by the mid-seventies, had become a consistent and splendid bowler. He began to attract the Test selectors as a bowler of great penetration and stamina. He was chosen for the tour of India and Sri lanka and was later to play in the Centenary Test in Melbourne.

In his first game for England at Delhi on that 1976–77 tour, he scored 53 and took 7 for 46 – it was the best bowling performance achieved by any England player on his Test debut.

In 1978, Lever topped the 100 wicket mark for the first time, taking 106 wickets at a cost of 15.18 runs apiece. He was the first Essex bowler to reach this mark for twelve years, and was named as one of Wisden's 'Five Cricketers of the Year'. He also won the coveted award among professionals of the 'Players' Player of the Year'. In fact, he won the award a second time, just going to show the great esteem that his fellow professionals around the country held for him as a man. When Essex beat Northamptonshire by an innings, Lever took 13 wickets in the match. In the Gillette Cup quarter-final match against Leicestershire, he took 4 for 27 off five overs to give him the 'Man of the Match' award in a game that was reduced to a ten over slog. He also took 5 for 36 against Lancashire at Old Trafford in a John Player League game.

In 1979 he topped the 100 wicket mark again, helping Essex to win their first trophy. At Ilford, he took 7 for 27 as Lancashire were bundled out for 84. He bowled the county to victory at Chelmsford against Leicestershire, taking 13 for 117. At Edgbaston against Warwickshire, he took another 13 wickets for 87; against Hampshire at Bournemouth, he took 7 for 40 as his superb form continued.

In 1980, he had his benefit season and from 1982 to 1985, he played for Natal in South Africa.

He began the 1983 season by taking 7 for 63 against Cambridge University but missed a great part of the summer when he had to undergo minor surgery. He returned to take 12 for 95 as Essex defeated Sussex by an innings at Hove. Against Yorkshire at Chelmsford, Lever took 7 for 78, reaching 100 wickets in an injury-affected season – it was a great performance and went a long way in helping Essex win the County Championship.

In 1984 John Lever became the first bowler to reach 300 wickets in the John Player League competition, beating Derek Underwood of Kent by just thirty minutes! In the County Championship Essex beat Lancashire by an innings, with Lever having match figures of 10 for 81. At Bristol he produced his career best bowling figures, taking 8 for 37 on a superb batting track, as Gloucestershire were bowled out for 90, Essex winning by 8 wickets. He was the first player in the country that summer to reach 100 wickets.

In 1986, he took 6 for 57 against Glamorgan at Swansea and won back his place in the England side, albeit for one Test against India at Headingley at the age of 37. In the second innings, he took 4 for 64, though England were well beaten. His pinpoint accuracy, which made him invaluable in limited overs games, helped him to take 5 for 21 against Somerset at Chelmsford in the John Player League.

He deservedly had a second benefit season in 1989, these only being awarded to the hardiest and best of performers, raising £135,596.

He had a rather disappointing last summer with Essex. He was involved in the last ball finish in the Benson and Hedges Final against Nottinghamshire and couldn't play in the Refuge Cup Final at the end of the season due to a recurrence of an old back injury.

After leaving Essex, he became sports master at a highly respected school in the county – Bancrofts School – and played Minor Counties cricket for Cambridgeshire, though Essex have retained his registration for first-class cricket.

John Lever had a great determination and will to win and was the complete professional; it being significant that his career coincided with the only trophies Essex have won in their history.

GEORGE LOUDEN

Born: 6 September 1885, Forest Gate
Died: 28 December 1972
Played: 1912 – 1927

FIRST-CLASS ESSEX RECORDS

Matches	Innings	NO	Runs	HS	Ave	100s
82	125	33	844	74	9.17	–

Runs	Wkts	Ave	BB	5wl	10wm	Ct
9,066	415	21.84	8/36	33	5	54

TEST MATCHES – 61

George Marshall Louden joined Essex from the Ilford Club, making his first-class debut in 1912, a season in which he could only play four matches. However, the following season he turned in some good performances and topped the Essex bowling averages with•18 wickets in five games. He displayed such promise that the experts of the time prophesied much success for him. He took 6 for 111 against Yorkshire, though Essex still lost and 4 for 28 as Lancashire were dismissed for 97.

Louden was a tall, strong pace bowler whose main asset was his accuracy. He stood over six feet in height and possessed a splendid physique. He had a high, easy action and could bowl very fast.

He was never reckoned to be much of a batsman, his highest score being 74 against Sussex at Leyton in that same 1913 season.

As a bowler, his best season was 1919 when he took 66 wickets, his best figures being 7 for 42 in Lancashire's second innings. Between 1919 and 1923 he played on a regular basis for the Gentlemen against the Players in fixtures at Lord's, the Oval, Folkestone and Scarborough.

In 1920 Louden only played in eight games, yet took 46 wickets, once again including the best analysis of the summer and what turned out to be his best analysis, 8 for 36 against Derbyshire at Southend. He didn't really play a full season, but in the years immediately following the First World War he must have been on the verge of Test selection. Louden worked in an office in the city and could never really spare the time to play cricket regularly, or perhaps more honours would have come his way. In 1921, When England had a torrid time against the Australians led by Warwick Armstrong, he wasn't one of the thirty players called upon to represent their country. This caused Sir Pelham Warner writing later about the disastrous Test series to comment that the omission of George Louden had been a mistake.

In 1921, playing in only seven games, he took 34 wickets, performing the hat-trick against Somerset at Southend, with his victims being R C Robertson-Glasgow, J J Bridges and S L Amor.

He headed the bowling averages in 1922 with 49 wickets in 7 matches. This included 13 wickets in the match against Sussex, with 8 for 48 in the first innings.

He had occasional days of inspiration the following season, the best of them giving him figures of 6 for 66 against Surrey in what was essentially a batsman's match. It has also been said that Louden dreaded playing for Essex when Johnnie Douglas was captain. Louden was a superb fast bowler, but often he had to bowl for thirty overs on the trot until he was completely exhausted!

In 1924 he took 42 Championship wickets, averaging 20.61, being in tremendous form against the South African tourists at the Garrison Ground, Colchester, taking 6 for 71. During the 1925 season he was only able to play in 8 matches, yet still topped the 50 wicket mark.

Louden played his last game for the county against Sussex in 1927, taking 1 for 78 and 4 for 32, helping Essex to win by 10 wickets.

Unhappily his career was relatively short and brought to an abrupt end by uncertain health, yet on his death on 28 December 1972, he had reached the age of 87.

ALFRED LUCAS

Born: 20 February 1857, Westminster, London
Died: 12 October 1923
Played: 1894–1907

FIRST-CLASS ESSEX RECORDS

Matches	Innings	NO	Runs	HS	Ave	100's
98	153	21	3,554	135	26.92	2

Runs	Wkts	Ave	BB	5wI	Ct
90	1	90.00	1/17	0	50

TEST MATCHES – 5

Alfred Percy Lucas was educated at Uppingham School, where he was without doubt, H H Stephenson's star pupil – a debt he never forgot, always saying how much he owed his teacher.

He was certainly good enough while still at school to play for the Gentlemen and though he didn't actually do so, he came very near to it. In 1874, the year he left Uppingham, he was chosen to represent the Gentlemen of the North v the Players of the South at Prince's and scored 48 and 23. He played the bowling of Morley and Shaw with great style.

On leaving Uppingham, he went up to Clare College, Cambridge where he won his Blue as a Freshman and was in the Cambridge XI for four years from 1875 to 1878. His top score in the four matches with Oxford was 74, topping the University averages in 1876 and 1877. He was a regular choice for the Gentlemen in their fixture against the Players, excelling in 1878 with 91 and then in 1882 with a fine 107, both matches being played at Lord's.

As a batsman, 'Bunny' Lucas had a classic technique and was so positive in his play of either foot that he seldom bored the crowd, though he was often described as a defensive opening batsman. He carried his bat through a completed innings on three occasions – for Surrey, MCC and Gentlemen.

At the Oval in 1880 with W G Grace, he shared Test cricket's first century partnership – 120 for the second wicket.

After playing for both Surrey and Middlesex he threw in his lot with Essex in 1889 with a view to helping his life-long friend, Charles Green.

He made his Essex debut on 31 May 1889 against the MCC at Leyton at the age of 32, scoring a forceful 103. he also hit a resolute 46 not out in Essex's first innings at Leyton in 1899, as they beat the Australians by 126 runs. In 1891 he hit 113 against Warwickshire in a rain-affected match, sharing in a second wicket stand of 168 with A S Johnson. In 1893, he scored 175 v Hampshire, adding 164 for the ninth wicket with T M Russell.

On 14 May 1894, he captained Essex's first match as a first-class county against Leicestershire.

The pressures of business prevented 'Bunny' Lucas from continuing as Essex captain when the side entered the 1895 season, in fact, he only played in four matches. One of these was against Somerset at Taunton, where Lucas played a great innings of 135 (one six and 18 fours) as Essex compiled 692.

He played his last county game for Essex in 1907 against Lancashire at Leyton, hitting 49 and sharing in a stand of 118 for the seventh wicket with Sam Meston. A few days later, he played his last match in Essex colours against the touring South Africans and bagged a 'pair'.

A most accomplished batsman, he did much to help the County Club as they moved into first-class status.

KEN McEWAN

Born: 16 July 1952,
Bedford, Cape Province, South Africa
Played: 1974–1985

FIRST-CLASS ESSEX RECORDS

Matches	Innings	NO	Runs	HS	Ave	100s
282	458	41	18,088	218	43.37	52

Runs	Wkts	Ave	BB	5wI	10wm	Ct
301	4	75.25	1/0	–	–	197

TEST MATCHES – 0

Ken McEwan was born in Bedford, Cape Province and educated at Queen's College, Queenstown. He was greatly encouraged by former England captain Tony Greig to come to England and join the Sussex ground staff. He played for the Sussex 2nd XI for two summers, though there was little hope of his being signed, as Sussex had more than their fair share of overseas players. He interested Northamptonshire and represented their 2nd XI also.

In July 1973 he was invited by Essex to play in a friendly at Perth against Scotland. He did well, and was immediately offered a three-year contract, which he accepted. Ken McEwan was a shy, nervous man and extremely popular with the fans and players alike. By the end of his first season in 1974 he had scored over a thousand runs and been awarded his county cap. All this after being given out lbw from the very first ball he faced in the County Championship against Nottinghamshire.

In 1976 he helped Brian Edmeades add 172 for the second wicket in the Benson and Hedges match against Minor Counties (East) at Norwich, hitting 116 in the process.

In the match against Sussex at Chelmsford in 1977, he hit the first double century of his career, a chanceless 218. On the Sunday following, he hit 104 in a John Player League game against Warwickshire and followed this with 102 and 116 at Edgbaston against the same county. Then, at Southend, he demolished the Gloucestershire attack with a blistering show of power in scoring 106 not out. He hit eight centuries that summer and ended the season in eighth place in the national batting averages and was chosen as one of Wisden's 'Five Cricketers of the Year'.

Against Northamptonshire at Ilford in 1978, McEwan and Gooch put on 321 for the second wicket. McEwan's innings of 186 lasted for four hours and contained a six and 26 fours. Also that season, he hit a masterful 133 against Nottinghamshire at Chelmsford in the Benson and Hedges Cup.

In 1979, at Edgbaston, McEwan blasted the Warwickshire attack all round the ground as he raced to 208 not out. His knock contained five sixes and 22 fours, Essex winning the match by an innings. Another exciting knock came against Derbyshire at Chelmsford. He hit 185 out of 239, his innings including three sixes and 29 fours. When Essex won the Benson and Hedges Cup that season, McEwan played a glorious innings of 72, with ten fours off 99 balls.

In 1980 McEwan missed the start of the season, being unwell, but returned to take 119 off the Leicestershire attack in a Gillette Cup match. After a spell out with an injury in 1981, he returned to the Essex line-up for the match at Canterbury, scoring 102. In the John Player League fixture against Middlesex at Chelmsford, McEwan hit a brilliant century, reaching three figures with a glorious hit into the pavilion. This season also saw him along with Brian Hardie add 120 for the fourth wicket against Leicestershire – an Essex record in the Nat West competition.

His cricket wasn't just confined to playing for Essex: he played for Eastern Province (1972–78) Western Australia (1979–81) and then joined Western Province in 1981 and played for them unti the end of the 1986 season.

In 1983 McEwan became the first batsman to reach 1,000 runs. He hit a ferocious hundred against Kent at Tunbridge Wells and eight all told over the season. By the end of the season, he had scored 2,176 runs at an average of 64.00 He helped Graham Gooch add 273 for the second wicket in a John Player League match against Nottinghamshire at Trent Bridge. His score in this match was 162 not out, the highest of his nine John Player League hundreds.

In 1984, McEwan became the first player to reach 2,000 runs for the season with a beautiful unbeaten 189 against Worcestershire. He savaged the Derbyshire attack for 101 and took a century off Somerset. His fourth century that summer was one I remember well at Old Trafford in the game against Lancashire. The red-rose side were dismissed for 229 and McEwan reached 95 in 75 minutes, eventually scoring 132 off 117 balls with four sixes and 13 fours – he was very close to scoring the season's fastest hundred. Essex bowled Lancashire out for 229 again in their second innings and won the match by 10 wickets.

In 1985, when Essex beat Nottinghamshire by 1 run in the Nat West Trophy Final, it was Ken McEwan's last appearance at a great cricket match. He ended on 46 not out, including one tremendous six off Saxelby, a cover drive into the Mount Stand.

After twelve glorious seasons with Essex, Ken McEwan decided to retire to his farm in South Africa. He could I am quite sure have gone on for another five years at least, but was tired of driving around the country without any prospect of playing Test cricket at the end of it.

He was a player of power and charm, bringing great pleasure into the lives of cricket followers up and down the country.

CHARLES McGAHEY

Born: 12 February 1871, Hackney
Died: 10 January 1935
Played: 1894–1921

FIRST-CLASS ESSEX RECORDS

Matches	Innings	NO	Runs	HS	Ave	100's
400	685	61	19,079	277	30.57	26

Runs	Wkts	Ave	BB	5wl	10wm	Ct
9,481	306	30.98	7/27	12	3	140

TEST MATCHES – 2

Charles Percy McGahey was a natural hitter in club cricket. He first appeared for the county in 1893, when the county was second-class. McGahey advanced slowly, but profited much from practice against professional bowling provided by Mr C.E. Green before each season at Leyton. His experience gained in match play also helped, and as his form improved, he became one of the best batsmen of his time.

In 1895, in the match against Somerset at Taunton, he hit 147, occupying the crease for three and a half hours, as Essex totalled 692 and went on to win by an innings and 317 runs. In his 15 matches that season, he scored 677 runs.

He was always getting into scrapes in his younger days and had little appreciation of the value of money.

In 1897 Charlie McGahey hit two hundreds in a week. At Hove, Essex reached 465, McGahey hitting 140; he then followed his performance with 123 at Leyton in the match against Leicestershire. Occasionally, his indifferent health threatened to cause his premature retirement from first-class cricket.

In 1898, McGahey's name became linked with Percy Perrin, following a third wicket stand of 191 against Lancashire. They became known as 'The Essex Twins' – they were of a similar build and were involved in a number of partnerships together. 'Twins' was an ironic description really, as the two men were quite different in almost every respect. In that match at Old Trafford, McGahey was the Essex hero with an innings of 145. It came in the fourth innings of the match and was made against the likes of Briggs, Cuttell and Arthur Mold. McGahey was certainly an extrovert character and was described by Home Gordon as 'a really fine vigorous bat and a fool only to himself: a good-hearted, light-hearted, excellent fellow'. He had a strong physique, but on the other hand he had a weak chest and was inclined to be consumptive.

For many years, McGahey, a bachelor, lived at the Three Blackbirds, a public house in Leyton. McGahey had a strong football connection and was a very useful full-back for Tottenham Hotspur, Arsenal, Clapton Orient and Sheffield United. He also captained the Middlesex and London representative teams.

McGahey, at a pinch, could spin the ball from leg (provided that it came down to earth) taking 330 wickets in all matches. In 1899 he missed his century by one run against Leicestershire at Grace Road, as Essex totalled 673.

He was a man noted for his wit and his liking of the odd drink. In a match against Somerset, McGahey was dismissed quite quickly and on his return to the pavilion, he was asked by a colleague who'd missed his dismissal what had happened. 'Bowled first ball by a bugger I thought died 300 years ago – Robinson Crusoe'. The name stuck and R C Robertson-Glasgow was 'Crusoe' ever afterwards.

In 1900, McGahey hit a century against Sussex at Leyton, putting on 235 in under three hours for the third wicket and then followed it in the same week by scoring 184, his highest score at the time, against Leicestershire. He also hit a sparkling century against Derbyshire at Derby and in all hit four hundreds that summer. His other hundred, 142 came against Kent at Leyton. He was a hard driver of straight deliveries, once driving the ball back so hard that he fractured his partner's arm! In that innings of 142 against Kent, he helped Percy Perrin put on 323, setting up what at the time was a world record for the third wicket.

McGahey started perhaps his most successful season, 1901 with innings of 77 not out and 125 against Sussex in the opening match. Altogether that season, he scored 1,838 runs at an average of 48.36 and a place in Archie MacLaren's side to tour Australia followed. McGahey set up an Essex record in that 1901 season, when he hit a century in each innings, 114 and 145 not out in the drawn encounter with Gloucestershire at Leyton. He was the first Essex player to hit a century in each innings of a match. His hundreds that summer, included one for London County against Warwickshire at the Crystal Palace.

Standing at around 6 ft 2 ins, McGahey played forward with great power and even used this stroke in defence of his wicket rather than wait to see what the ball might do. He was primarily a hitter, showing great strength in driving either to the off or on side. He very rarely cut, but would punish any short ball with severity. His play was such in that 1901 season that he was chosen as one of Wisden's 'Five Cricketers of the Year'.

Charles McGahey played only twice for England – at Sydney and Melbourne against Australia in 1902. He scored on these occasions, 18, 13, 0 and 7.

In 1904 McGahey and Carpenter put on 328 for the third wicket in the match against Surrey at the Oval, McGahey hitting 173. Also this season, he hit 225 against Nottinghamshire at Leyton.

McGahey who continued to score prolifically in 1905, hit the highest score of his career, 277 against Derbyshire at Leyton. Also this season, the Australian tourists lost their only game to a county side in a low scoring game; McGahey was Essex's top scorer in the match with 39! He headed the Essex batting averages with 1,645 runs, his highest total aggregate of runs. In 1906 at Llanelly whilst playing for an Essex XI, he hit the highest score of his career, 305 not out.

From 1907–1910, McGahey captained the County XI. In 1908 he showed his great power as a batsman, hitting a ball from Hallam the Nottinghamshire bowler over the Leyton pavilion and into the road! He also made the highest score of the 1908 season, 230 against Northamptonshire.

During the 1909 season, McGahey was hampered by an injury and only played in a few matches. At the end of the 1910 season, it was decided that a change of captaincy was necessary within the Club in an effort to revitalize the side. McGahey was in complete agreement and happy to stand down: he was replaced by Johnny Douglas. In 1912, it looked as though McGahey's form had begun to leave him, yet he and Perrin put on 312 in three hours for the third wicket in the match against Derbyshire at Leyton, McGahey scoring 150.

In 1913 he appeared in only 11 matches and the following season, the last before the War, he relinquished his post as assistant secretary and was awarded a testimonial. In 1921 at the age of 49, Charles McGahey played in his last first-class match, against Hampshire at Colchester – sadly he made 0 and 6.

Percy Perrin as I have said, was along with McGahey dubbed the 'Essex Twins'. He remembered one occasion when McGahey was on 99. He played at the next delivery, said 'Come one' but failed in his stroke and was bowled. As he passed by on the way to the pavilion, he said to the bowler, 'Lucky for you I wanted a drink'.

He was a 'paid amateur' as Assistant Secretary for a few seasons at £200 per annum and from 1930 to 1934 was official scorer for Essex. During this period, he recorded Yorkshire's historic opening partnership and was involved in the 'recount' which arrived at the finally accepted 555.

He died in Whipps Cross Hospital on 10 January 1935. His death was the result of an accident on Christmas Day when, slipping on a greasy pavement, he fell and damaged a finger. Septic poisoning set in and proved fatal.

Percy Perrin described him as 'one of the most popular and kindest-hearted players ever seen in first-class cricket'. Certainly no man gave more of his life to Essex cricket than Charles McGahey.

WALTER MEAD

Born: 25 March 1868, Clapton
Died: 18 March 1954
Played: 1894–1913

FIRST-CLASS ESSEX RECORDS

Matches	Innings	NO	Runs	HS	Ave	100's
332	469	125	3,843	119	11.17	1

Runs	Wkts	Ave	BB	5wI	10wm	Ct
28,423	1,472	19.30	9/40	117	30	151

TEST MATCHES – 1

Walter Mead was born at Clapton in Middlesex on 25 March 1868. The celebrated umpire Bob Thoms invited him to take part in a colt's match for the county of his birth, but he declined. He later moved to play as professional at Broxbourne Cricket Club and this move coupled with his residence in Essex gave him the necessary qualifications to play for that county.

He made his debut for Essex in the opening match of the 1890 season, against Surrey at the Oval. In the second innings, he bowled 37 overs and took 5 for 101. Later that season, in August, he played a major role in Essex's only win of the summer. It came in the fixture at Derby, Mead taking 6 for 27 in Derbyshire's first innings. Altogether that season, he took 33 wickets at a cost of 16.15 runs apiece.

In 1891 in the match against Leicestershire, Mead bowled 19.1 five ball overs and took 9 for 23, eight of his victims being clean bowled. He had been engaged as a bowler at Lord's and had become a bowler of great variety. Even at his medium-pace, he could make the ball turn sharply. Probably his most effective delivery was the leg-break, though he often hurried batsmen into their shots. At the end of the season, he had taken 76 wickets at an average of 13.16.

Mead was one of the most notable of slow-medium right-arm bowlers. He had a remarkable command of length and, possessing exceptional powers of spin, could make the ball turn even on the best of pitches.

In 1893 he took 17 wickets in a match for the first time. The opponents were Australia, Mead taking 9 for 136 and 8 for 69. At Sheffield this season, in the match against Yorkshire, when no other player exceded 20, Mead batting at number 10, hit an exciting 66 not out. He followed this up by taking ten wickets (4 for 8 and 6 for 73) – playing a leading part, as Essex romped home by 7 wickets. He played in three games for the MCC against both Universities, taking 26 wickets and finished second in the national bowling averages.

In 1894 he took 6 for 49 against Leicestershire in the first match Essex played as a first-class county. Against Oxford University he took 13 wickets and ended the season with 54 victims to his name.

Mead had his best ever season in 1895. He took 120 wickets for Essex and 179 wickets, including all first-class matches. It is a record that has not been beaten by an Essex bowler in the 96 years since. In the county's first victory in the County Championship over Somerset, Mead hit 33 and 35 not out and took 5 for 64 and 5 for 62 – a great all-round performance from a man who could always be relied upon to get both runs and wickets when they were most needed. Hampshire defeated Essex at Southampton by 171 runs, but not before Mead had taken 8 for 67 and 9 for 52. This bowling performance by Walter Mead is still the Essex record for the most wickets in a match. He followed this up with match figures of 12 for 103 against Leicestershire at Grace Road, the home side holding on, as rain came to their aid. They were 56 for 8 when the heavens opened. At the end of the summer he stood in fifth position in the first-class bowling averages. In fact, in three successive innings, he dismissed 24 batsmen for 192 runs.

In 1896, Mead played a great part in Essex's 7 wicket win over Leicestershire at Leyton. He hit a whirlwind 41 and took 14 for 132 in the match, including 9 for 75 in Leicestershire's second innings.

In 1899 Essex beat the Australians by 126 runs at Leyton, Mead taking 6 for 88 in the match. It was during this season that Mead played in his one and only Test. The game was at Lord's against Australia, Mead bowling 53 overs and despite 24 of them being maidens he took only one wicket for 91 runs. On the county scene though, he dominated the bowling, taking 146 wickets at a cost of 18.04 runs each.

In 1900 Essex drew their game with Sussex at Eastbourne, Mead taking 13 for 69 in the match. Also that season, Mead captured the best bowling figures of his career, 9 for 40 in the first innings of the drawn match with Hampshire. In fact, Mead took 9 wickets in an innings on three occasions, but just couldn't capture that elusive tenth. He ended the season with 122 wickets at 15.45 runs each.

Though Mead rarely performed brilliantly with the bat, he did hit 119 at Leyton against Leicestershire in 1902, to stun everyone. As a fielder he generally occupied the cover-point position with great distinction.

In 1903 Essex visited Surrey having lost their opening fixture to Yorkshire. Essex struggled to 187 and Surrey were 98 for 3 in reply when lunch was taken on the second day. In the afternoon session,

Walter Mead produced a magnificent spell of bowling to take 6 for 2 in the space of 33 balls and Surrey were all out for 107. Essex declared their second innings at 256 for 6, before Mead took 5 for 44 (to give him match figures of 12 for 78) and Surrey were all out for 76, Essex winning by 260 runs. Mead finished the season with 114 wickets at 14.60 runs apiece and was inevitably named as one of Wisden's 'Five Cricketers of the Year'. In the last game of that 1903 season, Mead destroyed Leicestershire taking 7 for 50 and 8 for 65; it was in fact his last game for Essex for two seasons.

Mead asked the Essex Committee for an increase in pay for the winter months. His request couldn't have come at a worse time for the Essex finances were at a low ebb – a view supported by Wisden, being regretful of Mead's actions. In fact, it alienated many of his close friends. Mead played for both the MCC and London County in his time away from Essex, but without much success, before returning for the 1906 season. He showed just how much he'd been missed, by taking 133 wickets at a cost of 10.18 runs apiece.

In 1907 Essex came very close to beating champions Nottinghamshire at Leyton, Mead bowling unchanged throughout the match with Reeves to take 12 for 73. He took 128 wickets in the season at an average of 17.02 and was by far the most successful member of the Essex attack. In 1911 he took 13 for 133 against Worcestershire at Leyton, including 8 for 35 in the first innings – it was the best performance of the season. The following season he was once again Essex's most successful bowler, taking 63 wickets at a cost of 25.50 runs each. In 1913, his last season for the county, he played in 12 matches and took 26 wickets: his last notable performance being 5 for 30 against Hampshire at Portsmouth in July. His 26 wickets cost 26.20 runs each, enabling him to finish the season in third position of the county's bowling averages. His last game was against Kent at Leyton. He only bowled one over, but hit a typically defiant knock of 21 not out. Walter Mead had the distinction of playing in a first-class match with his son and between the years 1891 and 1918 was a member of the MCC staff at Lord's.

He died in hospital at Ongar on 18 March 1954, a week short of his eighty-sixth birthday.

An outstanding right-arm slow-medium bowler, he was the mainstay of the Essex attack for almost their first two decades in the County Championship.

STAN NICHOLS

Born: 6 October 1900, Stondon Massey
Died: 26 January 1961
Played: 1924–1939

FIRST-CLASS ESSEX RECORDS

Matches	Innings	NO	Runs	HS	Ave	100's
418	664	66	15,736	205	26.31	20

Runs	Wkts	Ave	BB	5wI	10wm	Ct
34,201	1,608	21.26	9/32	108	22	279

TEST MATCHES – 14

Morris Stanley Nichols was born at Stondon Massey near Ongar on 6 October 1900, but for many years lived at Wickford. It was a great cricket enthusiast by the name of Dick Patmore who got the young Nichols a trial at Leyton. Stan Nichols came from farming stock and yet, in his early days, he wasn't even considered a bowler by the village team for which he played. When he was taken on the Essex ground staff, it was purely as a batsman. It is Percy Perrin who deserves most credit for converting Stan Nichols from a specialist left-handed middle-order batsman into one of the best all-rounders of the 1930s.

He made his debut for Essex in 1924 in the match against Yorkshire at Hull, securing his place on a regular basis the following season, when he took 52 wickets.

He took 110 championship wickets in 1926, producing some splendid all-round cricket. He passed the 100 wicket mark again the following season, when his batting too seemed to improve with each game. His best bowling performance in that 1927 season was 9 for 59 against Hampshire at Chelmsford.

In 1929 Nichols became the first Essex professional to complete the 'double' scoring 1,301 runs and capturing 104 wickets. He was to achieve this feat eight times, more than any other Essex player.

Although he never had an official tour of Australia, he went there with Gilligan's side that played 4 Tests in New Zealand. He impressed against South Australia at Adelaide, scoring 46 and 82 and taking 3 for 65. In New Zealand he opened with 9 for 108 and went on to head the Test batting averages with 92.50, due it must be recorded to several not out scores. Yet in all matches on that tour, he averaged over 43 with the bat and his 60 wickets cost only 15 runs apiece.

In 1930 he took 108 championship wickets at a cost of 19.50 runs apiece. He just missed the 'double' scoring 914 runs in all matches. When the Australians visited Leyton that summer, he took 2 for 23 and was chosen to play for England in the fourth Test at Old Trafford. In a rain-affected match (what else at Old Trafford) he took 2 for 33 and scored 7 not out. During the Colchester week in 1930, he took 16 wickets for 85 runs, the opponents being Somerset and Glamorgan. In all matches that summer, he took 121 wickets at 19.59 runs each, including 9 for 116 against Middlesex at Leyton.

In 1931, he again narrowly missed the 'double' scoring 872 runs and taking 97 wickets. He took 6 for 26 against Yorkshire at Headingley, including a hat-trick with the wickets of W Barber, E Robinson and A Wood. This must rank as the best performance of that season, although not in a statistical sense.

The following season he achieved the 'double' for the second time, taking 115 wickets at a cost of 24.92 runs apiece from almost 1,000 overs. He also scored 1,430 runs at 31.77. During the Chelmsford week in 1932, he took 21 wickets for 254 runs and scored 124 runs in three completed innings.

In 1933 Stan Nichols scored 1,406 runs in all matches, including three centuries: he backed this up with 114 wickets at 21.41 runs each (145 in all matches).

Although not selected for any of the Tests in 1934, he was 12th man on three occasions. He also played a great deal of representative cricket – it didn't affect his batting, he still passed the 1,000 run mark, but his bowling suffered, only taking 64 wickets.

In 1935 Nichols played an important role in the seven wicket defeat of South Africa. He followed his figures of 4 for 35 with a hard-hitting innings of 70. Lancashire were dismissed for 83 at Chelmsford, Nichols taking 4 for 14. However, the sensation of that 1935 season was the game between Yorkshire and Essex at Huddersfield. The Tykes hadn't lost a game since August 1934 but were shot out for 31 – at one stage they were 9 for 6. Nichols took 4 for 17 from 6.4 overs whilst 'Hopper' Read took 6 for 11. Essex too struggled and were 65 for 5 when Nichols produced a magnificent innings of 146 before falling to a catch by Hutton off the bowling of Bowes. Yorkshire didn't fare too much better in their second innings, being dismissed for 99 with Nichols taking 7 for 37 and Read 3 for 51. Without doubt, Nichols's performance of 146 runs (16 more than Yorkshire could total in two innings) and bowling figures of 11 for 54 was the greatest of his career. Nichols took his 100th wicket of the season in this match and again achieved the 'double' scoring 1,249 runs and capturing 157 wickets in all matches. His consistency that summer earned him selection for four Tests against South Africa, his best performance being 6 for 35 at Trent Bridge.

He had the great honour of being selected as one of Wisden's

'Five Cricketers of the Year' in 1933. That season, he was the first player in the land to reach 1,000 runs and 100 wickets.

In all matches in 1936, he scored 1315 runs and took 114 wickets to complete his fifth 'double' – it was also his benefit season. The following summer, he did the 'double' again scoring 1,247 runs and capturing 148 wickets in all matches played. In fact, he was the first player in the country to achieve this feat, as he had been in 1935 and 1936.

In 1938 Stan Nichols enjoyed his finest season, scoring 1,452 runs at an average of 35.41 and taking 171 wickets at a cost of 19.92 runs each. He had now cut down his run-up and not bowling as fast, but his effectiveness wasn't impaired. He was again the first player in the country to reach the 'double' and was chosen for the Gentlemen v Players match at Lord's. Nichols turned in a good performance with the ball against the visiting Australians, taking 6 for 25 in their first innings. At Gloucester that summer, Essex defeated the home side by an innings and 65 runs, Nichols having an outstanding match. He scored 159 out of Essex's total of 553 and then took 9 for 37 and 6 for 128. He dismissed Wally Hammond cheaply in both innings and at one stage in Gloucestershire's first innings, he had figures of 5 for 6 in five overs.

In his last season in first-class cricket, he still proved to be outstanding. He was by now 39 years of age, yet still the best player in the Essex line-up and the most exciting all-rounder in the country. He performed the 'double' again, scoring 1,387 runs and taking 121 wickets, again being the first player in the country to achieve this feat. In home matches he helped to demolish Derbyshire at Southend with 6 for 18 and 5 for 26 (all five victims being clean bowled); at Clacton he scored 80 and took 9 for 64 against Northamptonshire and in the away fixture at Hove against Sussex he scored a marvellous 146 and captured 8 wickets for 98.

He was chosen at the end of the season for the MCC team to visit India in 1939-40 but of course this was cancelled owing to the war.

Nichols was a great-hearted player: as a bowler, he was unfortunate to be at his best in an era of fast bowlers in this country. He was a very great cricketer and, not wishing to be detrimental to Essex, I'm sure if he had played for a more 'fashionable' club at the time, would have gained more international honours. His achievements in obtaining eight 'doubles' was an output only exceeded by Rhodes, Hirst, Jupp and Astill. Nichols was also a goalkeeper for Queen's Park Rangers and after the war, played as a professional in the Birmingham League.

If he had wanted it, Nichols could have secured a top coaching position as a player of great experience and reputaion.

He died at Neward in Nottinghamshire on 26 January 1961, aged 60.

Charles E. Green

The Right Hon. James Round

Frederick L. Fane

Charles J. Kortright

Alfred P. Lucas

Hugh G. P. Owen

Herbert A. Carpenter

Frederick G. Bull

Charles P. McGahey

Harding I. Young

William Reeves

Walter Mead

Percival A. Perrin

John R Freeman

Claude P. Buckenham

John W. H. T. Douglas

George M. Louden

Lawrence C. Eastman

Charles A. G. Russell

Jack O'Connor

Morris S. Nichols

Augustus B. Hipkin

James A. Cutmore

Alfred V. Avery

Raymond Smith

Paul A. Gibb

Trevor E. Bailey

Doug J. Insole

JACK O'CONNOR

Born: 6 November 1897, Cambridge
Died: 22 February 1977
Played: 1921–1939

FIRST-CLASS ESSEX RECORDS

Matches	Innings	NO	Runs	HS	Ave	100's
516	866	76	27,819	248	35.21	71

Runs	Wkts	Ave	BB	5wI	10wm	Ct	St
17,523	537	32.63	7/52	17	2	215	1

TEST MATCHES – 4

Jack O'Connor was 23 years old when he made his Essex debut in May 1921 in the match against Worcestershire at Leyton. He accomplished little in the four matches he played that year, but was to run into form rapidly the following year.

He was a right-handed batsman and spin bowler, the nephew of 'Bob' Carpenter and the son of John O'Connor who had played nine games for Derbyshire in 1900 as well as appearing for Cambridgeshire.

In 1922, Jack O'Connor hit the first of his 71 centuries for the county, it was at Northampton – a six and 13 fours in an unbeaten 102.

By 1923 O'Connor had begun to bat with the elegance and freedom that were to become his hallmark over the next sixteen years. In the match against Hampshire at Leyton, Essex needing 181 to win on a wicket of uneven bounce, were 16 short of victory with O'Connor on 99. After reaching his hundred with a single, he hit two fours in one over to clinch victory. His 111 not out from an Essex total of 183 was a masterly innings – it contained 18 fours and took him 170 minutes. In the following match against Gloucestershire at Cheltenham, O'Connor showed his fighting qualities, hitting 128 as he and Douglas put on 206 for the sixth wicket. It is a stand that has been equalled but never beaten. His next two scores were 93 and 99 to give him 431 runs in four consecutive innings at an average of 143.66.

O'Connor claimed a hat-trick at Worcester in 1925, where his leg-breaks bowled M K and H K Foster and then gave him a return catch off the bat of Gilbert Ashton. In all matches during the summer of 1926, O'Connor scored 1,402 runs and took 93 wickets, thus narrowly missing the 'double'. He followed this by taking ten wickets in a match on two occasions. The first came in 1926 against

Leicestershire at Grace Road and then the following summer when New Zealand visited Leyton.

In 1928 O'Connor reached the highest aggregate to date with 2,256 runs at an average of 47.44, including six centuries. He also took the most wickets for Essex that summer, 68 at a cost of 31.76.

Without doubt, in 1929, O'Connor was the most successful of all Essex batsmen. He scored 2,288 runs at an average of 44.86, hitting nine centuries. In his 116 against Kent at Folkestone, he scored 92 of his runs in boundaries – eight of these were consecutive scoring strokes.

He played for England 4 times, when a batsman's place in the side was probably at its most competitive – Les Ames, the great Kent wicket-keeper/batsman played 47 times for his country and scored over 3,000 runs, but never batted higher than No 7. O'Connor's highest Test score was 51 made against the West Indies at Kingston on the 1929–30 tour.

He followed his highly successful season by scoring 1,477 runs in championship matches in 1930 at an average of 43.44. He scored a century on five occasions, including two hundreds, 138 and 120 not out in the match against Gloucestershire at Bristol. In 1931 he put on 271 with Tom Pearce for the fourth wicket against Lancashire at Clacton.

In 1932 O'Connor suffered a bad injury at Old Trafford in the Test trial. He had his finger split by a ball from Harold Larwood that kept him out of the game for over a month. It was tragic, as O'Connor had shown outstanding form up to the middle of June, hitting 906 runs in 14 innings, including three hundreds. The following season saw him score 2,077 runs at an average of 44.19, his six centuries including a supreme innings of 237 against Somerset at Leyton. In 1934 he had his best ever season, scoring 2,350 runs in all matches with an average of 55.95, including nine centuries. This record is held jointly with Doug Insole; his run aggregate achieved in that year being an Essex record for fifty years, until Graham Gooch overtook it in 1984. His top score was 248 made in the match against Surrey at Brentwood, where he shared in a record fifth wicket stand of 287 with C T Ashton. Yet despite his outstanding performances, he wasn't selected for England that summer.

O'Connor again topped the Essex run-getters in 1935 with a total of 1,603 runs in all matches, though his batting average dropped somewhat. He continued in this vein the following summer, totalling 1,343 runs in all matches. In 1937 he headed their run-getters with 1,364 runs in championship games, but his average for the season was only 28.41. It was during this season that he helped R.M. Taylor put on 333 for the third wicket in the match against Northamptonshire at Castle Park, Colchester.

By 1938 he appeared to have returned to his best form, scoring

1,839 runs in all matches, including six centuries. He was the first professional to captain Essex which he did in the match against Somerset at Chelmsford this season.

In 1939 he scored 1,716 runs at an average of 37.30 with four hundreds. It was the fifteenth consecutive summer that Jack O'Connor had topped the 1,000 run mark.

He was an outstanding player of spin bowling and a fine driver and hooker but didn't always relish fast bowling. He was also an unusual right-arm slow bowler whose repertoire included both leg-breaks and off-spin.

O'Connor played for the London Counties along with Lawrie Eastman in 1940. In 1943 the Essex Committee instigated coaching classes for the youths under the watchful eye of Jack O'Connor being paid £6 for a week's coaching.

The Second World War had ended O'Connor's first-class career, but he coached first at Eton and later at Chigwell and for two seasons, 1946 and 47 appeared for Buckinghamshire.

Known as the 'Laughing Cavalier' his value to the Essex side was immense: he scored a century against all other first-class counties and also against both Cambridge and Oxford.

HUGH OWEN

Born: 19 May 1859, Bath
Died: 20 October 1912
Played: 1894–1902

FIRST-CLASS ESSEX RECORDS

Matches	Innings	NO	Runs	HS	Ave	100's
133	222	17	4,459	134	21.75	3

Runs	Wkts	Ave	BB	5wI	10wm	Ct
321	9	35.66	2/37	—	—	38

TEST MATCHES – 0

Hugh Glendower Palmer Owen was born at Bath, Somerset on 19 May 1859, yet his Christian names were indicative of Welsh extraction. He was educated privately and later at Corpus Christi Cambridge. Despite doing great things for his college, he was given little chance for the University side and didn't get a Blue.

Owen first played for Essex in 1880 at the age of 21. The following season he had his earliest success in county cricket. He played an innings of 51 for Essex against the MCC and Ground at Lord's, but his career as a county player really dates from 1885.

In 1882 he averaged 52 in 16 innings without obtaining his Blue. During that season, he hit an adventurous 44 for the Sixteen against the XI and was chosen for the match with the MCC at Cambridge. Unfortunately, he didn't do himself justice, scoring only 9 and 5 and wasn't tried again for the University.

His talents, however, were being recognized in 1884. The county's opening match of that summer was against Surrey at the Oval. Owen hit the county's top score of 69. *Cricket* commented – 'The play of Mr Owen in particular was deserving of the highest credit'.

In his first real season for the county, he scored an unbeaten 64 against Hertfordshire and 52 against Northamptonshire. In club cricket he did many notable things in 1885, playing for Bradwell and Tillingham and averaged 185 from six innings.

In 1887 playing for Trent College, where he was a master for nine years, he hit five centuries and totalled 1,809 runs for the season. During the following summer, he made 35, 104, 205, 31, 119, 55 and 23 in successive innings between 16 June and 19 July, being dismissed only once!

In 1889 Owen hit 1,839 runs and took 108 wickets with his right-arm medium-paced deliveries. That was also the year that he hit his highest county score for Essex, 153 out of a total of 295 made against Leicestershire at Leyton. Owen had gone in first and carried his bat. His hundred was the first made for the new Essex Club in county matches. He batted for a little over four-and-a-half hours, giving just two chances.

In 1890, playing for Trent College against Tibshelf in July, he carried his bat through both innings for 27 and 46. In one season, playing for Notts Forest Amateurs, his figures were quite remarkable:

Inns	No's	H.Sc	Runs	Average
5	4	61*	244	244.00

In 1894 only one first-class fixture was won in the county's first season as a first-class county, that being against Oxford University. Essex won by 9 wickets, Owen scoring the first century, 109. He headed the county's batting averages at the end of the season with an aggregate of 447 runs.

Owen was a fair-haired, large, rather clumsy man and a very steady batsman, but it was as a captain that he proved his capabilities. He took over the county captaincy from A P Lucas in 1895 and began with marked success. He was a very popular captain and certainly brought a sense of fun to Essex cricket. The first championship match that summer was at Edgbaston against Warwickshire. Owen led by example, scoring a well-hit 64, going on to top the batting averages at the end of the season with 21.00.

At one time, Hugh Owen was qualified to play for three counties – Somerset by birth, Derbyshire by residence and Essex by family home. Fortunately for Essex, he chose the latter.

In 1896 he hit a whirlwind 82 when Essex were 126 for 5 facing Leicestershire's 141. The following season under his leadership, the county climbed to third place in the championship. In 1902 the county only registered two victories and finished thirteenth in the championship. He only played in seven games that summer, but hit 134 against Hampshire at Leyton.

At the end of that season he stood down as captain, he was in his 43rd year. He was paid the warmest of tributes by Mr C E Green and presented with a gold watch and chain, scroll, gun and purse of 200 guineas. He led the county closer than anyone else for three-quarters of a century to the championship title.

A member of the MCC since 1885, Hugh Owen died at Landwyck, Southminster on 20 October 1912, aged 53.

TOM PEARCE

Born: 3 November 1905, Stoke Newington
Played: 1929–1950

FIRST-CLASS ESSEX RECORDS

Matches	Innings	NO	Runs	HS	Ave	100s
231	376	48	11,139	211*	33.96	20

Runs	Wkts	Ave	BB	5wI	10wm	Ct
927	15	61.80	4/12	–	–	144

TEST MATCHES – 0

Thomas Neill Pearce made his Essex debut under H M Morris against Sussex at Leyton in July 1929, scoring six. He was also, surprisingly, regarded as an all-round prospect and sent down 24 overs of medium pace but without a victim. He scored his maiden century, 152 against Lancashire in 1931 and headed the batting averages with 353 runs (Average 44.12) in six matches. The following summer, he headed the bowling averages, his six wickets costing 13.33 runs apiece.

Pearce agreed, at the beginning of the 1933 season, that he would act as captain for the first half of the season. The county finished in fourth place that summer, winning seven matches under Pearce's captaincy and six under Denys Wilcox who captained the county in the second half of the season. This was the county's highest position since 1897 and with more wins than ever before.

In 1934 Pearce scored 815 runs in 17 championship matches with his highest score being 111 against Worcestershire at Chelmsford.

He had another successful season in 1935, scoring 1,018 runs in all matches – it was the first time he'd passed the 1,000 run mark. He hit two centuries, including 105 against Lancashire at Chelmsford, made in the knowledge that his wife was undergoing an appendicitis operation in the hospital overlooking the Chelmsford Ground – Essex winning easily by ten wickets. In fact, Lancashire must have been Tom Pearce's favourite opponents – in all matches, he scored 687 runs in 12 completed innings, with four centuries and an average of 57.25. In the match against Northamptonshire at Colchester, he scored 97 not out, only hitting one boundary.

In 1936 he scored 714 runs at an average of 31.04, hitting 1,066 runs in all matches. His 1,000th run came in the Gentlemen v Players match at Lord's. It was the first time he'd been chosen for such a fixture and his last chance of reaching the four figure mark. His aggregate stood at 980, prior to this match, and after being dismissed for 1 in the first innings things didn't look too promising. However, in the second innings, he hit a brilliant 85.

He hit one century in 1937, failing by 61 runs to achieve a thousand for the season. During the winter of 1938 he informed the Essex committee that he would be unable to captain the side in 1939, owing to business commitments.

After the war he was, fortunately, able to resume the captaincy. His experience, temperament and consistent batting were never more necessary than in those first few post-war seasons. He had always been a sound batsman, but the war seemed to have improved him tremendously. He led the side from the front, scoring 1,332 runs with five centuries, as Essex finished in eighth position in the championship. Against Surrey, he hit 116 not out, Essex winning by an innings and 179 runs. Lancashire who finished third, also felt the power of Pearce's hitting as he took 140 off the red-rose attack, Essex winning by 15 runs.

He continued to lead Essex in the 1947 season, scoring 1,597 runs at an average of 45.62. In the match against Worcestershire at New Road, he hit 137 not out and 96, narrowly missing the distinction of hitting a century in each innings.

Though the county had a disappointing season in 1948, Pearce scored 1,825 runs at an average of 49.32, including four centuries. In the drawn match with Leicestershire at Westcliff, he hit a magnificent 211 not out. It was a chanceless innings, lasting over five hours and coming after Essex had been 71 for 5.

The year of 1949 proved to be Pearce's last solely as captain. He once again passed the 1,000 run mark and was also elected on to the Test selection committee. At the end of this season the Essex committee took the decision to appoint Doug Insole joint-captain with Pearce for the 1950 season, in order to give Insole the benefit of his experience. His duties as a selector, though, were taking up more of his time than he expected and he had to relinquish the position of joint-captain.

As a captain, Tom Pearce was always calm and good-natured. He could bring the best out of the side, being ideally suited both in temperament and in ability to take up the county captaincy. A popular man, he was in the main responsible for the rebuilding of Essex cricket after the war. In 1952 he was elected vice-chairman. At the end of that season, on the resignation of Hubert Ashton, he took over the reins as chairman, a position he held for 21 years. In his early years, Tom Pearce was a very keen Rugby player and in later life was to become famous as an international referee in the same sport.

In 1961–62 he was manager of the MCC tour of India, Pakistan and Ceylon. Tom was also wellknown for his work as honorary team manager for the Scarborough Cricket Festival and, in 1979, was deservedly awarded the OBE for his services to sport.

In November 1985, Tom celebrated his 80th birthday with a dinner in the Pavilion at the County Ground, Chelmsford. It was attended by players past and present, showing the great affection and importance Tom Pearce has in Essex cricket.

PERCY PERRIN

Born: 26 May 1876, Hackney
Died: 20 November 1945
Played: 1896–1928

FIRST-CLASS ESSEX RECORDS

Matches	Innings	NO	Runs	HS	Ave	100s
525	894	88	29,172	343*	36.19	65

Runs	Wkts	Ave	BB	5wI	10wm	Ct
740	16	46.25	3/13	–	–	284

TEST MATCHES – 0

Percival Albert Perrin, 'Peter' to his close friends was born in Hackney and had trials with Middlesex, playing for their 2nd XI. He was a natural cricketer, gaining a lot of experience playing club cricket in Tottenham. He made his Essex debut in 1896 in the match against Surrey at the Oval, when two weeks short of his twentieth birthday. He had to face Tom Richardson, Bill Lockwood and Tom Hayward (who topped the Surrey bowling averages that season) but still battled hard to score 52.

Perrin regularly went in first wicket down and in that first season he hit 50 against the Champion County, Yorkshire, Essex winning by 4 wickets. Later that summer, he hit his maiden century for the county, 139 against Warwickshire at Edgbaston. He also made the first of his many notable partnerships with Charles McGahey, when they added 111 for the third wicket against Leicestershire at Grace Road. At the end of his first season, Perrin possessed the county's highest aggregate of runs, 719, only captain H G Owen having a better average.

As a batsman, he could dominate any attack and was at his best against fast bowling. In his early years, fast bowlers often put three or four fielders in the deep to try to stem Perrin's driving. He relied heavily on forward play until, later in his career, he acquired the ability to combat the best spin bowlers by using defensive strokes of great power. He earned himself the title of 'the best batsman never to have played for England'.

In 1899 he was in fine form throughout the season and scored 1,491 runs in all matches, including six centuries. Against Kent at Leyton in 1900, Perrin hit 205 before being caught in the deep: it being his first double hundred.

In 1902, when Essex were dismissed for 64 by Middlesex at Lord's, Perrin showed his fighting qualities by ending the game on 38 not out. In 1903 he was credited with a hundred in three consecutive innings, including 170 and 102 not out in the match against Nottinghamshire at Trent Bridge.

In the match against Derbyshire at Chesterfield in 1904, Perrin scored 343 not out from Essex's total of 597 in their first innings. He hit 68 fours, the law still existing that a six could only be scored when the ball was hit out of the ground – it was alleged some years later, that 14 of his boundaries would now have been classed as sixes. His superb knock compared favourably to Lancashire's Archie MacLaren, who hit 62 fours in his record 424 made against Somerset at Taunton. Perrin's innings remains the only triple century ever made by an Essex player in County cricket – and as unbelievable as it may seem, Essex lost!

In 1905 Perrin hit a hundred in each innings, 140 and 103 not out in the match against Middlesex at Lord's, the second coming against the clock to win the match for Essex. At the end of the season, he was chosen as one of Wisden's 'Five Cricketers of the Year'.

Perrin was the leading batsman again the following season, when he scored 1,893 runs, which at the time was an Essex record.

Percy Perrin was always reliable as a batsman, scoring over

1,000 runs in 18 seasons. He hit 66 three-figure innings, all for Essex except one made for the Gentlemen of the South against the Players of the South in 1907 – out of a total of 211.

However, Perrin couldn't field. He was heavy on his feet and couldn't move quickly to the ball. He certainly had a safe pair of hands and a long reach, but his inability to move at great speed, prevented him from ever appearing for his country, though it must also be said that he was at his prime in the golden years of English batting.

In 1911, a new captain was chosen. It should have been Percy Perrin who at the age of 35 was Essex's leading batsman – it was obvious though that the Essex Committee were determined that the position should not go to Perrin. The new captain was Douglas and Perrin, in his first game under his leadership, hit a hundred to save the game against Middlesex. At the end of that 1911 season, he had scored 1,281 runs at an average of 51.24, including six centuries. Two of these came in the match with Nottinghamshire at Trent Bridge, Perrin scoring 112 and 100 not out. He headed the batting averages again the following season, scoring 1,009 runs in all matches; his top score being 245 made against Derbyshire.

After the First World War Perrin was 43 but still had a few years of batting in him. In 1919, he scored 126 and 101 not out against Kent at Leyton.

He finished his active cricket career with a well hit 51 made against Oxford University at Colchester in 1928. He was, by this time, 52 years of age and reappeared in the Essex side as captain, though he practically retired three years earlier.

Percy Perrin possessed a very keen knowledge of the game and could fully appreciate a player's ability. It was said of him, 'he doesn't often speak, but when he does, it's worth listening to'. With this in mind, he was elected to the Test selection committee, becoming chairman in 1939.

He was a real personality, spectators watching him with great admiration and interest. He maintained an active interest in cricket right up to his death at Hickling in Norfolk on 20 November 1945.

NORBERT PHILLIP

Born: 12 June 1948, Bioche, Dominica
Played: 1978–1985

FIRST-CLASS ESSEX RECORDS

Matches	Innings	NO	Runs	HS	Ave	100s
144	201	22	3,784	134	21.13	1

Runs	Wkts	Ave	BB	5wI	10wm	Ct
10,638	423	25.14	6/4	18	1	45

TEST MATCHES – 9

Norbert Phillip had played cricket for both the Windward Islands and the Combined Islands since 1969, but despite his obvious ability as a hard-hitting batsman and quick bowler, he found it very difficult to break into the West Indian Test team. Essex had tried to register Richard Hadlee (now Sir Richard) for the second half of the 1977 season, but when the TCCB would only sanction such action if a three-year contract was offered, Essex turned their attentions to Norbert Phillip. It is generally accepted that Phillip himself made the first tentative approaches. He was obviously very keen to further his career, both in England and at Test level and he arrived at Essex as a completely unknown player.

Phillip represented the West Indies in nine Tests between 1977–78 and 1978–79. His best performances with both bat and ball coming against India, 47 and 4 for 48.

In his first season with Essex, 1978, he helped to bring a memorable victory at Gloucester, hitting a magnificent 134. It was a maiden century of awesome power. His hundred arrived in 112 minutes and contained 7 sixes and 12 fours. Coupled to this, Phillip was a quick and hostile bowler.

There were many occasions in his career with Essex where Phillip was to plunder the opposition attack. He launched a great attack on the Northamptonshire bowlers in the Benson and Hedges Final of 1980, but couldn't quite snatch victory in the last over, being at the non-strikers end for the majority of it. In the same season, he took the Surrey attack and fellow West Indian Sylvester Clarke in particular apart, though as the scores were tied and Essex had lost more wickets in this one-day game, Surrey won.

In 1981 he hit 66 off 25 balls to bring victory over Warwickshire. Later in the same season he hit 83 off 74 balls as Essex won on a slow wicket at Milton Keynes. Again in the Sunday League, Essex and Surrey were involved in a strange affair. The umpires had ordered 39 overs per side due to a short delay for rain. Phillip and Stuart Turner smashed their way to a quick 51 run partnership when at 4.10 pm they came off the field, only to find that they had to return to fulfil the umpires' wishes and bowl the 39th over. Phillip hit 19 runs off this 'extra' over bowled by Roger Knight. He ended with an unbeaten 80, twice hitting balls from Knight onto the Surrey pavilion.

Phillip played for the Windward Islands from 1969 to 1985, the last four seasons as captain. His best performance being 7 for 33 against the Leeward Islands at Roseau in 1981.

In 1982 in a game I remember well, Phillip took 6 for 13 against Lancashire at Old Trafford in the John Player Sunday League.

On the first day of the match against Surrey at Chelmsford in May 1983, play was washed out. On the second day, Essex totalled 287, leaving Surrey with just an hour to bat. They were dismissed for 14 inside 15 overs with Norbert Phillip taking 6 for 4! His actual figures were:

O	M	R	W
7.3	4	4	6

Later in the season, Phillip completed the first hat-trick of his career in the match against Northamptonshire at Wellingborough. He was only in the side because Derek Pringle had broken a finger – his victims were Steele, Mallender and Griffiths.

Norbert Phillip was a good player and played a very important role in the first years of Essex's latter day success.

KEN PRESTON

Born: 22 August 1925, Goodmayes
Played: 1948–1964

FIRST-CLASS ESSEX RECORDS

Matches	Innings	NO	Runs	HS	Ave	100s
391	460	165	3,024	70	10.25	–

Runs	Wkts	Ave	BB	5WI	10wm	Ct
30,288	1,155	26.22	7/55	37	2	344

TEST MATCHES – 0

Discovered by Alf Gover, Ken Preston was given a trial by Essex towards the end of the 1947 season. He had a nice easy action but under the expert tuition of Gover, he was able to increase his pace and master the art of swerve.

He made his first-class debut for Essex in 1948, picking up 42 championship wickets at a cost of 28.83 runs each. His best performance being 6 for 85 against Worcestershire at Clacton. He was looked upon as a great prospect, but unfortunately in January 1949 he broke his left leg playing football. It was a blow both to Essex and England, for he was coming good at a time when the national side were short of fast bowlers. The leg mended early enough for him to play 2nd XI cricket later that season, but he didn't play at first-class level.

He returned to play in the 1950 season, but still hadn't fully recovered from his injury. In fact, he was never to bowl as quick as he'd bowled in the summer of '48. The following summer though, he showed a complete recovery, taking 79 wickets in a season, when he never missed a match.

By 1953 Ken Preston had shortened his run-up somewhat and it paid dividends, as he took 91 wickets. At the start of the following season because the county had a surfeit of seam bowlers, Preston often found himself in the 2nd XI. He terrorized the Minor County batsmen, topping the averages of that competition. When he did return to the first team, he was a better bowler for his experience. He had developed a more than useful leg-cutter and this coupled with far greater accuracy than in previous seasons saw him go on to take 94 wickets in the County Championship at a cost of 24.97 runs each.

He seemed to be improving every season and in 1955 crept even closer to the 100 wicket mark, taking 96 wickets at 23.19 runs apiece.

In 1957 he had his best season yet, taking 140 wickets at 20.35 runs each. He performed well in matches against Middlesex (5 for 42) and Leicestershire (4 for 16) helping Essex win both fixtures with these performances in the second innings as their opponents chased victory.

The following summer of 1958 saw Ken Preston miss the 100 wicket mark by just one, claiming 99 victims at a cost of 23.67 runs each. He also showed his ability as a fine fieldsman, taking 38 catches in the season, three more than the previous year.

He picked up yet another injury in 1959 and had to miss part of the season, though he still went on to claim 60 wickets. His benefit match against Gloucestershire this season ended in a tie. The 1960 season saw Preston fully fit and bowling well, taking 73 wickets. In the match against Lancashire at Southend, Preston had match figures of 7 for 70 and shared in a 9th wicket stand of 58 with Trevor Bailey as Essex won by 9 wickets. In the match against Leicestershire at Hinckley, Essex won by an innings and 27 runs, Preston returning match figures of 8 for 59.

In 1961 he took 88 wickets at a cost of 27.36 runs each, bowling particularly well against Derbyshire, taking 4 for 28 in their second innings as they chased a small total.

Ken Preston was widely respected in the game – a player of great determination. He was also an extremely popular player and became the first secretary of the Essex Supporters' Club.

In 1962 Preston took 80 wickets, including 12 for 85 in the county's win over Lancashire at Leyton. In 1963 he took fewer wickets, 58 and at a slightly higher cost. His career came to a close the following summer – this great servant of Essex cricket having taken 1,155 wickets between the years of 1948 and 1964.

DEREK PRINGLE

Born 18th September 1958, Nairobi, Kenya
Played: 1978–

FIRST-CLASS ESSEX RECORDS

Matches	Innings	NO	Runs	HS	Ave	100s
167	225	41	4,550	128	24.46	3

Runs	Wkts	Ave	BB	5wI	10wm	Ct
11,141	452	24.64	7/18	18	2	82

TEST MATCHES – 21

Derek Raymond Pringle was born in Nairobi, Kenya, the son of D.J. Pringle. He shares a family record with the Amarnaths and Hadlees in that his father played for East Africa in the 1975 World Cup; sadly he was killed in a car crash shortly afterwards.

He impressed with the ball in those early years, taking all ten wickets when representing the Nairobi Schools Under 13½.

On moving to England, he attended the Felsted School and later Fitzwilliam College at Cambridge University.

He made his Essex debut in 1978 and then gained his Blue in each of the years from 1979–82. In 1979 against Oxford as a freshman, he scored a century and took 5 wickets – not many freshmen in the history of the match have done as much. His form at Cambridge was such that he was selected to make his Test debut for England in 1982, during the last of his four summers at Fenner's. It was a move of imagination and originality to choose Pringle. His figures at county level for Essex were at this stage of his career, mediocre but he had performed exceptionally well with both bat and ball for Cambridge. In fact, to play in his second Test, he had to give up the honour of captaining the Light Blues at Lord's and let them beat Oxford University without him.

He showed himself eager to learn on leaving Cambridge, having yet to prove himself in the county game. He was the only Essex player chosen to tour Australia in 1982–83, yet he returned a much better player.

He hit his maiden first-class hundred in the County Championship in that 1983 season against Hampshire at Southend. In 1984 he took 5 for 35 at Chelmsford in the Benson and Hedges Cup match with Lancashire and then against Warwickshire, after Essex had followed on and set the Midland county 155 to win in 56 overs. He took the last four Warwickshire wickets to give Essex an amazing win. He revelled in the conditions at Canterbury to take 9 for 108 in the match, including a beautiful spell of bowling in the first innings to claim 7 for 53. He also took nine wickets in the match against Middlesex at Lord's, including 6 for 66 in the first innings. Against Worcestershire in the John Player League he hit an unbeaten 77 and bowled tightly to take 1 for 19 from his alloted eight overs.

He was now developing into a highly-intelligent all-rounder. In his University days he was a hard-hitting stroke-player, but has become more restricted, often sacrificing his personal achievements for his team's needs. He is a right-arm medium-fast bowler with a good action and is able to extract awkward bounce.

In 1985 he and Ken McEwan set a new Essex record for the third wicket in the John Player League with a stand of 190 against Warwickshire at Edgbaston, Pringle hitting an unbeaten 81. He produced three hauls of 5 wickets in one-day games: 5 for 41 against Gloucestershire in the John Player League, 5 for 12 against Oxfordshire and 5 for 23 against Middlesex, both in the Nat West Trophy.

The following season, he hit his highest score at Test level, 63 against India at Lord's. He produced good figures in two home County Championship fixtures, 5 for 65 against Hampshire at Ilford and 7 for 46 at Chelmsford against Yorkshire.

In 1988 he hit the highest score of his first-class career, 128 against Kent at Chelmsford and for the second time (he took 5 for 108 at Edgbaston in 1984) he took five wickets in an innings for England against the West Indies, taking 5 for 95 at Headingley.

In 1989 he was the joint leading wicket-taker with Steve Watkin of Glamorgan with 94 first-class wickets. It was against Glamorgan this season, that he produced his best figures with the ball, 7 for 18.

The Essex batting was so good in 1990 that he had to wait until mid-July before he had his third first-class innings. He did hit an unbeaten 77 off 38 balls (with 4 sixes and 6 fours) against Scotland in the Benson and Hedges Cup, and a quick-fire 84 at Grace Road in the Championship.

Derek Pringle has matured into a high-class all-round cricketer. He could be the ideal replacement for Graham Gooch as Essex captain, if he decides to relinquish the post.

WILLIAM REEVES

Born: 22 June 1875, Cambridge
Died: 22 March 1944
Played: 1897–1921

FIRST-CLASS ESSEX RECORDS

Matches	Innings	NO	Runs	HS	Ave	100s
271	422	34	6,451	135	16.62	3

Runs	Wkts	Ave	BB	5wI	10wm	Ct
16,137	581	27.77	7/33	37	5	115

TEST MATCHES – 0

William Reeves was born in Cambridge, later joining the ground staff at Leyton, where his life was centred, for he had married into the family of Edward Freeman, the Essex head groundsman who had played occasionally for the county.

He made his county debut in 1897, though it was rather a mild introduction, he scored four runs and bowled just three overs for 12 runs. The following season he topped the county bowling averages, though it must be said he only took 11 wickets!

By the turn of the century he was given much greater opportunity and began to show distinct promise as both a hard-hitting batsman and a right-arm medium-pace bowler.

Some of his best bowling performances were at Leyton, which at this time was considered a batsman's paradise. In 1901 he took the last five Derbyshire wickets in eleven balls, without conceding a run.

He strove hard to fill the gap left by Walter Mead's departure and in 1904 he had his best season with the ball, taking 106 wickets at a cost of 16.16 runs apiece. The following season of 1905 saw Reeves fall away somewhat as a bowler, taking only 44 wickets, but it was a season when he produced his best form with the bat. He hit two centuries in his 1,174 runs (average 29.35); one of these being a superb 135 (his highest score) against Lancashire in a little under two hours. His other century, 101, was made against Surrey, both matches being played at Leyton. He also punished the powerful Yorkshire side that summer, hitting 71 out of 90 in 50 minutes with Charles McGahey as his partner. Essex totalled 521 and the County Champions had to follow-on. They only just escaped defeat, having three wickets in hand. The last pair at the wicket were Lord Hawke and Ernest Smith, who stayed over an hour without getting a run.

Reeves hit his only other hundred for Essex in 1906. He scored 104 against Sussex, as he and Claude Buckenham (68) put on 163 for the eighth wicket in only 70 minutes – a superb performance. In 1907 Reeves and Walter Mead bowled unchanged through both innings of Nottinghamshire who came out tops in a low-scoring game by just seven runs. They went on to win the County Championship without losing a match.

By 1909 he had recovered some of his lost form with the ball and took 7 for 79 against Yorkshire at Leyton, as he hit a superb 71 out of a stand of 89 in just 45 minutes. In 1919 he and George Louden put on 122 for the last wicket in the match against Surrey. In 1920, Reeve's penultimate season, he took 62 wickets and found something of his old zest despite being 45 years old.

William Reeves was also a member of the Lord's ground staff for many years. He represented the MCC in quite a few matches, his best performance for them coming at Lord's in 1920, when he dismissed five Nottinghamshire batsmen for only 13 runs. In 1921, his last season of first-class cricket, he was given the match against Middlesex as his benefit.

After playing his last game for Essex, he became one of the best first-class umpires. He stood in many Test matches and often gave evidence of his humour in this capacity.

A notorious fast bowler was continually appealing. Reeves remarked, 'There's only one man who appeals more than you do'. 'Oh, who's that?' asked the bowler. 'Dr Barnardo', came the reply. Once a batsman protested that he was never out, Reeves replied 'Weren't you? Wait till you see the papers in the morning'.

Reeves was also involved in the later stages of his life in the coaching of schoolboys at Lord's.

In 1939, at the ripe 'old' age of 64, he made a successful appearance in an Essex XI against Forest School, taking several wickets.

A most useful batsman and bowler and one of the best first-class umpires, William Reeves died after an operation on 22 March 1944.

JAMES ROUND

Born: 6 April 1842, Colchester
Died: 24 December 1916
Did not play first-class cricket for Essex

Born at Colchester on 6 April 1842, he was educated at Eton College where he soon gained a reputation as a most effective long-stop and bowler of both fast round and slow under-hand.

He was in the Eton XI with both Hon. C C Lyttleton and R A H Mitchell, the ruling spirit of Eton cricket. Against Harrow in 1860, he made 0 and 20, following it with 5 and 22 in the match against Winchester.

Moving on to Oxford, he developed into the best amateur wicket-keeper of the day and led the Christ Church XI. However, whilst at Oxford, he didn't receive his blue, though he did represent the Gentlemen against the Players whilst still in residence.

He made four appearances for the Gentlemen, with his most successful being that at the Oval in 1867. He scored 29 and had a hand in the downfall of eight opponents, catching three and stumping two batsmen and only allowing one bye. Also that year, he scored 142 for Southgate v Oxford University on the Magdalen Ground.

In 1868 he became a barrister and began his political career when he was elected Member of Parliament for Colchester. He had been a member of the MCC since 1865 and served on the Committee from 1869 to 1871.

Despite his parliamentary duties, he found an opportunity to devote a great deal of time to assist the club in its formative years. He chaired the public meeting held at the Shire Hall, Chelmsford on 14 January 1876 and was Chairman of the Essex Club until 1882. In addition he was captain of the club between 1876 and that year. Of course, during that time, there would have been comparatively few matches played and Round would not have had difficulty in obtaining time off from his parliamentary duties to lead the side.

James Round died at his home at Birch Hall on Christmas Eve 1916, aged 74. His contribution to the game of cricket had been immense, playing an important part in driving Essex into the first-class game.

'JACK' RUSSELL

Born: 7 October 1887, Leyton
Died: 23 March 1961
Played: 1908–1930

FIRST-CLASS ESSEX RECORDS

Matches	Innings	NO	Runs	HS	Ave	100s
379	628	51	23,610	273	40.91	62

Runs	Wkts	Ave	BB	5wI	10wm	Ct
7,480	276	27.10	5/25	5	–	280

TEST MATCHES – 10

Albert Charles Russell was born close to the then Essex county ground at Leyton on 7th October 1887. After a lifetime of being listed as 'A C ' statisticians now call him 'C A G.' due to a discovery on his birth certificate years after his death. He was the son of Tom Russell, who was for many years the Essex wicket-keeper. When he was a youngster, he had often played truant from school in order to watch his father play for Essex.

He made his debut for Essex in 1908 aged 20, but didn't make his first 50 until 1911. It wasn't easy during that period to break into a team that contained amateurs such as Douglas, Fane, McGahey and Perrin and the professional Carpenter. However, Russell and Essex persevered and by 1913, 'Jack' Russell's batting began to raise the highest hopes. After missing the opening game that summer, he played in the other 17 games, proving himself to be both capable and consistent. His maiden first-class hundred came in the game against Hampshire at Leyton, when he hit 102, helping Colin McIver put on 210 for the first wicket. In the last game of that season, he hit a brilliant 110 at Old Trafford against Lancashire, thus becoming the only Essex batsman that season to reach 1,000 runs in county matches. He ended the season with 1,072 runs at an average of 34.58.

He had gained a great deal from the coaching and advice from 'Bob' Carpenter and was gradually becoming one of the greatest of all Essex batsmen.

Russell was a master of the on-side strokes, occasionally driving well to the off, though many spectators didn't find his play attractive to watch. He certainly wasn't a negative player and was one of the most dependable batsmen in the game.

In 1914, in the match against Leicestershire, he and McIver again put on 212 for the first wicket. It was at the time a county record,

Russell hitting yet another century and passing 1,000 runs for the season. Also this season he helped 'Bob' Carpenter put on 237 for the second wicket against Worcestershire.

He was the leading batsman in the first season after the war, scoring 1,387 runs, including four centuries. It wasn't long after this that his batting was being noticed in quarters outside Essex. In 1920, for the Players against the Gentlemen, he hit a superb 93 in the company of Hendren, Hobbs and Woolley. He was the first Essex player to pass 2,000 runs in a season and was rewarded with a place on the MCC tour to Australia. Surprisingly in that 1920 season, he only hit three centuries and only seven were made by Essex in the season. Russell's consistency, however, is emphasised by his 17 fifties.

During that winter tour of Australia in 1920–21, he hit 135 not out and 59 at Adelaide in the third Test. His century was the highest score in the series for England. The Australians followed England back to this country, but Russell wasn't called upon until the fourth Test, when he hit 101. He followed this in the next Test at the oval with an unbeaten 102 in England's second innings.

In 1921 Essex won only five matches. One of these was a 132 run victory over Worcestershire, Russell hitting 151 in Essex's second innings of 500 for 5 dec. Northamptonshire were a county to suffer at the hands of Russell that summer. He hit 108 in the game at Northampton, following it with the highest score of his career, 273 in the return game at Leyton. His innings took him four-and-a-half hours before he was finally stumped. When Essex entertained Lancashire at Leyton that summer, Russell and Loveday put on 191 and 104 respectively in opening each innings. During that season of 1921, Russell scored 2,236 runs and was second only to Hampshire's Philip Mead in the national batting averages.

His best year, without doubt, was 1922 when he put together an aggregate of 2,575 runs – the highest of all batsmen, including 9 centuries, for an average of 54.78. He hit 172 against Northamptonshire (again!) as he and Perrin put on 207 in two-and-a-quarter hours for the second wicket. When Essex played Surrey at the Oval, Russell hit two separate hundreds in a match for the first time, scoring 115 and 118. He also made five appearances in total for the Players against the Gentlemen, his best innings of 162 coming at Lord's that season.

Not surprisingly, he was named as one of Wisden's 'Five Cricketers of the Year' and was selected for the side to tour South Africa, captained by Mann.

He was England's leading player in South Africa that winter, topping the Test averages with 436 runs at an average of 62.28. In the final Test, England batted first and scored 281, of which Russell made 140. South Africa were then dismissed for 179, Russell taking a brilliant catch at slip to dismiss South Africa's danger man

Herbie Taylor. Russell had by this time been forced to take to his bed, but when England were struggling at 26 for 4, he returned to score 111 and help A.E.R. Gilligan add 92 for the tenth wicket, a record in England v South Africa matches. He became the first Englishman to score two centuries in a Test – this has been commemorated in two ways, by a plaque in the Chelmsford pavilion and by the planting of a tree at the Kingsmead ground in Durban.

There can be few first-class batsmen whose last three scores in Test matches were 96, 140 and 111, but 'Jack' Russell was so ill on his return to England that Essex had to send him away for a recuperative holiday in the spring. He was never to play Test cricket again. His ten appearances saw him score 910 runs for an average of 56.87, including five centuries.

In 1923 Russell again scored most runs for Essex, 1,159 but was in poor form early in the season, following his illness in South Africa. In 1925 he scored seven centuries and narrowly missed two thousand runs, scoring 1,942 runs at an average of 48.55. During this 1925 season, he hit 135 not out against Gloucestershire to win the match for Essex, after being dropped before he had scored. In 1927 he shared in his second three-figure opening partnership in two innings, putting on 122 and 140 with the Rev F H Gillingham against Surrey at the Oval. In 1928 he hit eight centuries in his 2,243 runs and averaged 64.08. The following season, he missed the 1,000 runs for the first time for many a year, but his appearances were limited by a coaching engagement. In 1930, his final season for Essex, Russell scored 1,355 runs, including four centuries. He took part in 16 stands of 200 or more for Essex, the biggest being 263 with Dudley Pope against Sussex at Hove that summer of 1930. He also scored 98 and 93 in his very last match against Sir Julian Cahn's XI at West Bridgford.

He enjoyed the distinction of hitting centuries against every first-class county.

Following his retirement from first-class cricket, he was first a coach and then a groundsman. He was also among those professional players granted honorary membership of the MCC. Additionally, he stood as a first-class umpire for several seasons.

He was one of an unlucky band of cricketers born in the late-Victorian era, who lost four years to the hostilities of World War One.

Russell was a batsman for all occasions. If an Essex innings needed a straight bat, Russell provided it and if a run chase was needed for victory or declaration, it was Russell who would lead the charge for runs. 'Jack' Russell is fourth in the all-time list of Essex run-getters, after Fletcher, Perrin and O'Connor, having scored in fewer matches and at a better average.

He died at Whipps Cross Hospital on 23 March 1961, aged 73.

PETER SMITH

Born: 30 October 1908, Ipswich
Died: 4 August 1967
Played: 1929–1951

FIRST-CLASS ESSEX RECORDS

Matches	Innings	NO	Runs	HS	Ave	100s
434	647	115	9,652	163	18.14	8

Runs	Wkts	Ave	BB	5wl	10wm	Ct
42,314	1,610	26.28	9/77	117	27	330

TEST MATCHES – 4

Thomas Peter Bromley Smith made his debut for Essex in 1929, appearing in five matches, his solitary wicket costing 233 runs. He was at this early stage in his career, a medium-pace bowler. In 1930 he took 85 wickets, including 12 in the match against Worcester at Leyton. He repeated this haul the following season, though at a slightly higher cost.

He demonstrated over the next couple of seasons that his leg-break skills had developed tremendously and, in 1933, he took 100 wickets for the first time. It was in 1933 that he suffered a cruel hoax, when he was asked to report to the Oval, having been told that he had been selected to play for England against the West Indies. Thirteen years later he did appear for his country at the Oval, against India. In 1934, he shared in a ninth wicket stand of 113 made in only 90 minutes against Yorkshire with Adam Powell the former Cambridge University wicket-keeper. In 1936 Essex defeated the Indian touring team at Brentwood by seven wickets. During the course of this game, Peter Smith hit a century and shared 12 wickets with cousin Ray. He also put on 214 with Jim Cutmore for the eighth wicket in this match.

The following summer he took most wickets, 155 at an average of 19.60 and earned recognition in being invited to tour India with Lord Tennyson's team in the winter. His best match that season was against Northamptonshire at Colchester, where his figures were 7 for 56 and 6 for 62.

In 1938, Peter Smith took 144 wickets at a cost of 24.36 runs each. He also performed well with the bat, scoring 846 runs in all matches, including two centuries. It was during this summer of 1938, that he was chosen for the Gentlemen against the Players at Lord's. He responded by taking 4 for 140 and 5 for 68 against the Gentlemen.

In the last season before the war, Smith just missed 100 wickets, taking 95 at a cost of 20.69 runs apiece. He was chosen for the MCC team to visit India in the winter of 1939–40, which of course was cancelled owing to the hostilities.

During the war years, he played some cricket against top class opposition at Alexandria during his Army service in the Middle East.

In 1946 he took 11 for 119 in the match against Surrey at the Oval. He took 120 wickets at a cost of 19.49 runs each, backing this up with 834 runs – a useful start for this pre-war stalwart, and but for absence through injury would probably have completed the 'double'. He took 5 wickets in 15 balls for 1 run against Northamptonshire at Brentwood. Northamptonshire were all out for 106 after the first wicket had put on 96! Essex also claimed a notable victory that season against Lancashire at Old Trafford. Chasing 299 to win, the red-rose county were dismissed for 283 with Peter Smith taking 7 for 75. He was also chosen for the third Test against India and was selected for the MCC touring team to visit Australia in the winter of 1946–47.

In 1947 Peter Smith took 172 wickets (more than any Essex bowler had taken before) at a cost of 27.13 runs each. He also scored 1065 runs at an average of 23.66 – an extremely good season. In fact, he bowled 1,606 overs that summer, more than any other bowler in the country. On ten occasions he bowled more than 45 overs in an innings and at Trent Bridge sent down 63 overs costing 203 runs. On eighteen occasions over a hundred runs were scored off his bowling in an innings. He took 16 for 215 against Middlesex at Castle Park, Colchester, taking 9 for 77 in the first innings.

He also helped set another Essex batting record in the game against Derbyshire at Chesterfield in the summer of 1947. After feeling unwell, he came in at number 11 to join Frank Vigar. They proceeded to put on 218 for the last wicket, after Essex had been 199 for 9. Peter Smith scored 163, the highest score ever made by a number 11 batsman; his innings including 3 sixes and 22 fours. Not surprisingly, he was chosen as one of Wisden's 'Five Cricketers of the Year'.

He'd also taken 9 for 121 when representing the MCC against New South Wales, being the only bowler who has ever taken 9 wickets in an innings for MCC in Australia.

In 1948 he took 92 wickets, not being as successful as usual! He followed this in 1949 with 82 wickets – was he on the decline? His 1948 figures included 9 for 108 against Kent at Maidstone and 9 for 117 against Nottinghamshire at Southend.

The following season of 1950 was the worst in the County's history. They finished bottom of the Championship table with only four victories, yet Peter Smith returned to something like his old self, taking 237 wickets at 27.14 runs each. Peter Smith occasionally bowled without a run-up in order to catch his wicket-keeper unawares. It didn't happen too often when Tommy Wade was behind the stumps, because Wade was a useful wrestler and his brother reputed to be the best in England!

In 1951 he took 80 wickets in County Championship matches. At the end of the season, he announced his retirement after a most successful career that had begun 22 years earlier.

He took 3 wickets in 4 balls on three occasions, but failed to take a hat-trick. He was an extremely accurate bowler and could make the ball dip in flight. He was also capable of bowling out good batsmen on good wickets. He possessed a high wrist-spinner's action and his leg-spinners and occasional googly brought him 1,610 wickets for Essex.

Peter Smith died from a brain haemorrhage following a fall whilst on holiday in France in 1967.

He was a great figure in the history of Essex cricket and was a most popular player wherever he went.

RAY SMITH

Born: 10 August 1914, Boreham
Played: 1934–1956

FIRST-CLASS ESSEX RECORDS

Matches	Innings	NO	Runs	HS	Ave	100s
419	646	81	11,125	147	19.69	6

Runs	Wkts	Ave	BB	5wI	10wm	Ct
39,817	1,317	30.23	8/63	73	10	179

TEST MATCHES – 0

Making his Essex debut in 1934, Ray Smith, cousin of Peter Smith, turned in some useful performances before the war. In 1938, he took 54 wickets, though his best season before the war was 1939 when he took 79 wickets at a cost of 20.68 runs apiece.

Ray Smith was a dynamic batsman and a fast-medium bowler who could also revert to off-breaks when the occasion demanded.

During the war he represented the British Empire XI in matches that were organized regularly. He also captained an Essex XI against the British Empire XI at Chelmsford which raised £148 17s 5d for King George's War Fund for Sailors. Ray Smith was also a member of the Middlesex and Essex side in their annual fixture with Kent and Surrey at Lord's.

109

In 1946 Ray Smith began as he had finished before the war, scoring 729 runs and capturing 116 wickets at a cost of 25.49 runs each. When Essex played the Indian tourists at Southend, he took 6 for 56 as India were bowled out for 138. He showed signs of becoming a natural successor to Stan Nichols. At this time, he would start as a fast-medium bowler, turning to bowl his off-breaks later in the innings. It was this willingness that led to a gradual bowling into the ground of a player who was at that time potentially one of England's finest fast bowlers.

In 1947 Ray Smith achieved the cricketers 'double' scoring 1,386 runs at an average of 28.87 and the unenviable record of the most costly hundred wickets in a season – 125 at 37.26 runs each. He bowled more overs, 1,557 than anyone in the country, except for his cousin Peter! However, this season he enjoyed himself with the bat at the expense of Gloucestershire. In three consecutive innings against them, he scored 51 in 40 minutes at Westcliff (including 16 in an over from Tom Goddard) 63 in 37 minutes in the second innings of that fixture and 51 in 25 minutes (including 10 fours) in the return match at Bristol.

In 1948 he scored 112 against Derbyshire at Colchester, reaching his maiden century in 63 minutes – the fastest hundred of the season. He was the only Essex bowler to take over 100 wickets, though he was still suffering the effects of over-bowling. At Ilford, Surrey scored 469, Ray Smith having the remarkable figures of 4 for 75 in 47 overs! A show of amazing steadiness in such a long innings.

In 1949 he took 100 wickets for the fourth successive season and in 1950, which proved to be the worst season in the County's history, he performed the 'double' scoring 1,149 runs (average 23.40) and capturing 102 wickets at a cost of 34.77 – the only Essex player to do so.

Along with his cousin Peter, the Smiths would often dominate a match. Against Kent at Maidstone in 1950 Ray bowled 59 overs and took 6 for 202, whilst Peter bowled 65 overs and took 4 for 190, Kent being bowled out for 532 in 152 overs.

Ray Smith just missed achieving the 'double' in 1951. He scored 1,294 runs and took 95 wickets in all matches. When Essex entertained South Africa at Ilford that summer, he hit the season's fastest hundred. Sent in early, he reached his fifty in 40 minutes, his hundred in 70 minutes and was eventually dismissed for 147 in just 94 minutes – all this out of an Essex total of 204. When Nottinghamshire visited Clacton, Ray Smith backed up a fine knock from Doug Insole with a hard-hitting innings of 82, before being stumped, to give Essex first innings points.

In 1952, Ray Smith once again did the 'double' scoring 1,045 runs at an average of 24.30 and capturing 136 wickets at 28.87 each. He bowled 423 overs more than any other Essex bowler and took

54 more wickets than his nearest rival this season. Along with Trevor Bailey, these were the only two players on the county circuit to perform this feat.

At the end of that season it was reported that Ray Smith had received a three-year offer to play for Accrington Cricket Club in the Lancashire League. The Essex Committee decided to offer him a three-year contract with a testimonial in the third year, and a further three year option if the county wanted to keep him. In 1953 he once again took 100 wickets, bowling more overs than anyone else. In 1955, he hit another century in quick-time, 73 minutes against Northamptonshire at Wellingborough.

His last season of first-class cricket was 1956, when he took 58 wickets. He often had to bowl round the wicket to have any chance of gaining an l.b.w. decision, as his in-swingers moved so much. He was a great club man and a fine cricketer but one who never played for his country. Perhaps his attitude towards Essex County Cricket Club can be summed up by his remark 'I would give a month's salary if we could beat Yorkshire'.

BRIAN TAYLOR

Born: 19 June 1932, West Ham
Played: 1949–1973

FIRST-CLASS ESSEX RECORDS

Matches	Innings	NO	Runs	HS	Ave	100s
539	901	69	18,240	135	21.92	9

Runs	Wkts	Ave	BB	5wI	10wm	Ct	St
21	1	21.00	1/16	–	–	1,040	191

TEST MATCHES – 0

English cricket hadn't gathered momentum after the war years and the *London Evening News* for their part, introduced a coaching scheme and schoolboys were invited to apply. Brian Taylor was one of three who found their way into first-class cricket this way. He had played for Essex and London Schools, the latter side captained by England manager Mickey Stewart.

In 1949 he went straight from school on to the Essex staff when Tom Pearce was captain and Tom Wade was wicket-keeper. He made his first-class debut that season at the age of 16 against Cambridge University at Fenners on 7th May. After making his debut, he had to do his national service and so the county signed Paul Gibb from Yorkshire.

In 1954 an injury to Paul Gibb gave Taylor his first real chance in the senior eleven and this he grasped with both hands. As well as deputizing capably as a wicket-keeper, Taylor showed such promise as a forcing left-handed batsman that after Gibb returned, he often appeared in the Essex side by virtue of his batting abilities. It wasn't really until 1956 that Brian Taylor became the regular keeper for Essex. He dismissed 75 victims and scored 1,259 runs in all matches at an average of 26.22. He also hit his maiden century, 127 against Glamorgan at Cardiff, and was awarded his county cap. He was chosen by the Cricket Writers' Club as the 'Best Young Player of the Year' and to cap it all, at the end of the season, he was selected to tour South Africa with the MCC under Peter May's leadership.

In 1957, Taylor had another good season, scoring 1,311 runs and dismissing 83 victims, yet throughout the season he had 11 ducks! In 1958 Taylor had 75 victims (64 caught, 11 stumped). He had a disappointing summer with the bat, but bounced back in 1959 to score 1,837 runs at an average of 30.61: it was his best season as a batsman. He continued his good work behind the stumps, taking 72 victims (60 caught, 12 stumped). It was during this season that he hit the highest score of his career, 135 against Middlesex at Lord's. It was an innings that contained two sixes and 22 fours and went a long way in helping Essex defeat Middlesex.

In 1960, whilst his form behind the stumps had fallen away somewhat, his batting kept him in the side and he scored 1,358 runs in all matches at an average of 27.16, playing some match winning innings.

Taylor broke the Essex record for the number of wicket-keeping dismissals in 1962: a season with 79 catches and 10 stumpings. His batting wasn't up to scratch, though he did score a match-winning century against Gloucestershire, including three sixes and 15 fours and captured 5 victims for the first time.

The following season Taylor just missed scoring his 1,000 for the season by 5 runs, averaging 24.26 with the bat. In 1964 he scored 1,225 runs at an average of 27.22 and his wicket-keeping was as good as ever. In 1965 he again just missed the 1,000 run mark, scoring 929 runs and, though the 1966 season was a disappointing one for the county, Taylor scored 1,264 runs at an average of 22.98.

At the beginning of the 1967 season it was decided to invite Brian Taylor to captain the Essex 1st XI for the following summer. He was Essex's first professional captain and took over a side of mainly young players which was to form the nucleus of the successful Essex team of the late seventies and eighties. It was a very difficult time for this now 35 years old hard-hitting wicket-keeper batsman to take over. The revival of Essex cricket in Taylor's first year as captain did not materialize. Wisden commented: 'Taylor did not satisfy everybody with his handling of the side, and certainly more than one of his declarations proved difficult to understand; but he probably profited from experience during his first season as captain'.

The financial crisis that had hit the Essex club meant that Brian Taylor was to operate with just a staff of 12, including himself – yet this was to give the Club its strength. Brian Taylor taught his talented and promising yet mostly untried cricketers to be professional. He insisted on standards of dress and fitness. Earlier in his life, he had been a noted footballer, playing amateur football for Dulwich Hamlet and later as a professional with Brentford, Bexley and Dover and so he brought about a course of pre-season physical training. The Essex side became the most exciting fielding side in the country with everyone working for each other.

In 1968 he took his one and only first-class wicket against Northamptonshire, but was at his best behind the stumps. In 1970 against Leicestershire at Grace Road, he dismissed 8 players in the match.

The honour of hitting Essex's first century in the John Player League fell to 'Tonker' – he took 100 off 81 balls in 95 minutes against Derbyshire at Buxton. he had the nickname 'Tonker' because of his ability as a hard-hitting batsman. He once forced Les Jackson of Derbyshire to bowl the opening over of the innings with four fielders on the leg-side boundary!

In July 1972 he was forced to miss the Essex match with Kent at Maidstone. It was the first match he'd had to miss since coming into the championship game against Middlesex at Lord's in 1961 – a run of 301 consecutive appearances for the county. At the end of the season, he was chosen as one of Wisden's 'Five Cricketers of the Year'.

In 1973, which was Taylor's last season, he had become a Test selector and missed eight matches. At the end of August at Chelmsford, he played his 539th and last match for Essex against Nottinghamshire. He took five catches and a stumping in the match and passed Herbert Strudwick's record of 964 catches in county championship matches. As a wicket-keeper, his appeals in home matches could be heard all round the county!

Upon his retirement from first-class cricket, after a spell with a public relations company and one selling provisions, he set up his own sports goods company.

He remained active in cricket long after his first-class retirement in 1973. He captained the Essex 2nd XI until 1981 and from 1979 to 1985 was the coach at Cambridge University.

Brian Taylor took over the Essex side when morale in the club was low, but he left them on the threshold of honours. He was an excellent wicket-keeper and a most attractive left-handed bat: his services to his County are immeasurable.

STUART TURNER

Born: 18 July 1943, Chester
Played: 1965–1986

FIRST-CLASS ESSEX RECORDS

Matches	Innings	NO	Runs	HS	Ave	100s
354	503	98	9,264	121	22.87	4

Runs	Wkts	Ave	BB	5wI	10wm	Ct
20,987	810	25.90	6/26	27	1	215

TEST MATCHES – 0

Stuart Turner was born in Chester but educated at Epping Secondary School. He made his debut for Essex in 1965 but was 'released' before being recalled in 1967.

In 1968 he hit his maiden first-class century against Glamorgan at Ilford, helping Robin Hobbs add 192 for the eighth wicket in two hours – a sensational stand.

In 1970 coming in at 67 for 6 in the match against Somerset at Taunton, Turner hit 121 out of 163 in three hours, the highest score of his career. It was during this season that Turner won a regular place in the side for the first time. His brisk medium-pace bowling brought him 65 championship wickets and his county cap.

In the opening match of the 1971 season he performed the hat-trick against Surrey, his victims being Storey, Long and Jackman.

In 1972 he returned what were at the time his best figures in first-class cricket, 5 for 39 against Somerset. When Essex entertained Middlesex at Chalkwell Park in mid-July, the men from Lord's wanted 216 to win and at 108 for 1 looked handily placed. Turner then took 3 for 0 in 11 balls and gave Mike Brearley a hard time – the Middlesex side just about hung on for a draw. It was after this game that Brearley commented on the improvement of Stuart Turner as a bowler.

In 1974 in the match against Glamorgan at Swansea, Essex were 202 for 9 when Acfield joined Turner who was on 31. They stayed together for 133 minutes and 42 overs adding 122 for the last wicket – Turner finishing on 118 not out. It was Turner's only hundred in an outstanding summer. He hit 963 runs and took 73 wickets in all matches. He also won the Wetherell Award as the country's leading all-rounder, emulating Keith Boyce's feat. Turner also came close to selection for the England tour to Australia, being high in the selector's minds. He was certainly unlucky not to have gained representative honours of some sort because of his natural all-round ability – yet he developed into a seasoned performer.

In the John Player League matches of 1975, Essex decided to experiment and open the innings with Turner. His highest score in this position was 87 as Essex were defeated by Worcestershire, when the last pair were at the wicket and only four balls remained.

In 1976 he took 78 wickets in county championship matches alone. In 1977 he took 77 first-class wickets, bowling with his usual endeavour and producing his career best figures, taking 6 for 26 against Northamptonshire at Northampton. Turner was also the leading wicket-taker in the John Player League, claiming 22 victims.

Turner began the 1979 season in fine style. In Essex's opening match against Kent he hit 102 in 110 minutes with five sixes and nine fours. In the match against Northamptonshire he took 5 for 70 and 5 for 5: it was the only time in his career that he took ten wickets in a match.

In one-day cricket his nagging accuracy and selective hitting and ability in the field, made him invaluable. In 1986 at Southchurch Park, Southend, Stuart Turner received a plaque during the game against Worcestershire from the Association of Cricket Statisticians to commemorate his achievement on becoming the first player to score 3,000 runs and take 300 wickets in the John Player League, but he was to play in only one more Sunday game after this award.

Turner announced his retirement from the first-class game at the end of the 1986 season. He had been one of Brian Taylor's 'magnificent twelve' and yet in his early days, at county level, he had been told that he wasn't good enough. He played for the rest of his career, twenty years, proving those people wrong!

FRANK VIGAR

Born: 14 July 1917, Bruton, Somerset
Played: 1938–1954

FIRST-CLASS ESSEX RECORDS

Matches	Innings	NO	Runs	HS	Ave	100s
256	397	62	8,660	144	25.58	11

Runs	Wkts	Ave	BB	5wI	10wm	Ct
8,958	236	37.95	8/128	8	–	195

TEST MATCHES – 0

Frank Vigar was a tall, ungainly, yet very determined right-handed batsman and leg-break bowler. He made his first-class debut for Essex in 1938, showing much promise. In 1939, he hit his maiden first-class century against Gloucestershire at Chalkwell Park, Westcliff. The Somerset born all-rounder was sent in as night-watchman to save the wicket of Jack O'Connor. He went on the next day to score 121 and save Essex from following on – O'Connor was dismissed from the very first ball he faced the next morning!

During the war year of 1944, a West of England XI was formed and Frank Vigar was one of its leading lights.

After the war he made a very confident start to first-class cricket. In 1946 he scored 753 runs and took 51 wickets with his leg-breaks. He made 44 and 43 in his two innings against Sussex at Brighton, batting for well over five hours in the process. He also held five catches in an innings in two matches that summer, against Middlesex at Westcliff and Northamptonshire at Brentwood.

In 1947 Vigar hit 1,735 runs, including five centuries. In the match against Derbyshire at Chesterfield, he and Peter Smith set a new record for the Essex tenth wicket. When Smith joined Vigar, the Essex total stood at 199 for 9. They put on 218, Peter Smith hitting 163, the highest score ever made by a No. 11 batsman, Frank Vigar scored 114 not out.

During the game with Derbyshire in 1948, Vigar scored 94 in an eighth wicket stand of 152 with Ray Smith, occupying the crease for over four hours.

Probably the unhappiest match of Vigar's career was the visit of Australia to play Essex at Southend. Tom Pearce brought on Vigar with his gentle leg-spin for the last over before lunch in an attempt to lure Don Bradman into a reckless stroke. In fact, not a single ball of the over touched the ground, the Don simply went down the track and cracked the first five balls over the boundary to various parts of the ground, the sixth he hit extremely hard, but straight to mid-off. To cap it all, Frank Vigar suffered a 'pair' though he did end up with 2 for 66.

In 1949 Frank Vigar scored 1,449 runs and performed well with the ball, taking 7 for 102 against Somerset, though Essex lost by an innings and 50 runs. The following season he once again passed the one thousand mark, scoring 1,020 runs and taking six catches in the match against Nottinghamshire at Ilford.

He held five catches in an innings for the third time against Surrey at the Oval in 1951.

At the end of the 1954 season, the Essex Committee decided to terminate his engagement.

He was a very useful all-rounder; a tall, thin, very capable and solid batsman, a very good close to the wicket fielder and a more than useful leg-break bowler.

TOMMY WADE

Born: 24 November 1910, Maldon
Played: 1929–1950

FIRST-CLASS ESSEX RECORDS

Matches	Innings	NO	Runs	HS	Ave	100s
318	472	135	4,972	96	14.75	–

Runs	Wkts	Ave	BB	5wl	10wm	Ct	St
1,391	47	29.59	5/64	1	–	413	177

TEST MATCHES – 0

A Maldonian, Tommy Wade began his career as an off-break bowler, taking 4 for 11 against Nottinghamshire at Colchester and then 5 for 64 at Chelmsford in the match against Somerset. Also at Chelmsford, he and Roy Sheffield put on 110 for the last wicket against Warwickshire. It was Sheffield whom Tommy Wade was to replace as a wicket-keeper in 1938.

In 1936 Wade was involved in another profitable last wicket stand, as he and Ken Farnes added 149 in the match against Somerset at Taunton.

During the 1936–37 tour of Australia by the MCC, Tom Wade kept wicket in two matches, when both the regular keepers, Les Ames and George Duckworth were injured. He just happened to be visiting Australia at the time and was awarded an MCC touring cap for his appearances.

By 1938 Wade was the established wicket-keeper and was most capable of scoring runs when the occasion demanded. It was to be his best season behind the stumps, claiming 78 victims (62 caught and 16 stumped). In the match against Surrey at Westcliff he took 7 victims (6 caught and 1 stumped). He also showed his ability as a fine wicket-keeper at Colchester in the match against Kent. Kent scored 742, Wade only conceding two byes, and the first of those didn't appear until the score had reached 626!

In 1939 he continued to keep wicket at a high standard, backing this up with 736 runs at an average of just under 20.

Tom Wade was also a keen all-in-wrestler. The Essex Committee didn't raise an objection as long as it didn't interfere with his services to the County Club.

He took 76 victims in 1947, with exactly half of his victims stumped. His best performance came in the match against Lancashire at Clacton, Wade claiming 6 victims (4 caught and 2 stumped) in the Lancashire first innings.

Towards the end of the 1948 season Tommy Wade unfortunately developed fibrositis and had a prolonged absence due to this. His popularity was shown by the public response to his benefit. He netted over £3,000 – which was a record for an Essex professional.

At the end of the 1950 season Tommy Wade retired. He was a large man and was noted for his trademark – a series of finger exercises before each ball was bowled. He was also well known for his shriek-like appeal on the field of play and as a practical joker off duty.

HARDING YOUNG

Born: 5 February 1876, Leyton
Died: 12 December 1964
Played: 1898–1912

FIRST-CLASS ESSEX RECORDS

Matches	Innings	NO	Runs	HS	Ave	100s
128	186	50	1,413	44	10.38	–

Runs	Wkts	Ave	BB	5wI	10wm	Ct
9,092	368	24.70	8/54	18	3	59

TEST MATCHES – 2

Harding Isaac Young was born at Leyton and achieved early prominence in minor cricket while serving in the Royal Navy. As he practised at Leyton, the excellence of his bowling in the nets attracted the attention of Mr C.E. Green who had captained Essex between 1883–88. He must have been greatly impressed for he bought Young out of the Service to play for Essex. From this originated his nickname 'Sailor' by which he was known throughout the cricket world.

He made his first-class debut for Essex in June 1898 in the game against Derbyshire at Leyton, going on to take 19 wickets during the season.

The following season of 1899 was, undoubtedly, Young's best. He took 139 wickets at a cost of 21.79 runs apiece and made 607 runs. When Essex played Warwickshire at Edgbaston, Young had a match analysis of 15 for 154, including 8 for 54 in the second innings.

When Essex entertained the touring Australians at Leyton, they gained one of their greatest victories. 'Sailor' Young played his part to the full. It was Essex's first game of the season and when Young joined Lucas, Essex were 144 for 9. In a little over half-an-hour, the last pair had added 55, Young's share being 33. The following day, Australia were dismissed for 144, Young bowling Trumper for 0 and going on to take 4 for 42. Essex too found the going hard, though McGahey (39) and Turner (54) put on 93 for the fourth wicket. The Australians were left to make 200 to win on the third day. It was thought that they would win, but certainly not easily. The Australians were bowled out for 73, Young taking 7 for

32, ably supported by Walter Mead who took 3 for 32. Wisden made the comment: 'Young won the match for Essex on the Saturday morning and at the same time establishing his fame as a bowler. He was practically unplayable, pitching outside the off stump and turning the ball in six or eight inches with his arm.'

He also played in two Tests in 1899 against Australia, taking six wickets in each match. His best bowling being 4 for 30 at Headingley; his 12 Test wickets costing 21.83 runs each. He also hit 43 at Old Trafford in his second game: surprisingly, he was never selected again.

He also represented the Players against the Gentlemen on two occasions. In that glorious summer of 1899 at the Oval, he helped Tom Hayward add 135 for the last wicket, hitting the highest score of his career, 81 in the process: he also took 7 for 141 in the match. His second appearance for the Players came the following season at Scarborough. During this season he began to decline as a great bowler, though he did return to take 70 wickets in 1901, albeit at quite an expense.

'Sailor' Young dismissed 10 or more batsmen in a match on three occasions and in 1907 he performed the only hat-trick of his career against Leicestershire at Leyton. The game itself was ruined by rain, Young's victims being A.E. Knight, lbw S. Coe, bowled and V.F.S. Crawford, caught behind the wicket. Young's full analysis was 4 for 6.

Whilst classed as an all-rounder, his strength certainly lay in his bowling. He was a left-arm bowler of medium-pace from a good height and with what was described as a 'deceptive curl' or 'confusing swerve'.

Young suffered from muscular rheumatism and was unable to play regularly, though he did tour the West Indies in 1910–11. He was on the ground staff at Lord's for a long time and often turned out for the MCC. From 1921 to 1931 he served as a first-class umpire and then until a very late age, he was engaged in coaching schoolboys.

A player whose rise had been quite spectacular, 'Sailor' Young died in hospital on 12 December 1964, aged 88.

APPENDICES

Statistical Analysis

Whilst it is purely a matter of opinion as to how good a player a man is, or has been, and it is certainly true that figures seldom tell the true story of any cricket, the author hopes the following will go some way to explaining why he has chosen the following eleven players as his team of 'Essex Greats':

1. G A Gooch
2. P A Perrin
3. J O'Connor
4. K W R Fletcher (Captain)
5. C P McGahey
6. T E Bailey
7. M S Nichols
8. J W H T Douglas
9. B Taylor
10. C J Kortright
11. W Mead

ESSEX TOP TENS

The following section lists the best performances in each of several categories, showing in statistical form the 'top ten' for Essex.

Most Matches
1. K W R Fletcher — 572
2. B Taylor — 539
3. P A Perrin — 525
4. J O'Connor — 516
5. T E Bailey — 482
6. J W H T Douglas — 459
7. G Barker — 444
8. L C Eastman — 442
9. J K Lever — 439
10. T P B Smith — 434

Most Catches
1. K W R Fletcher — 517
2. B R Hardie — 346
3. K C Preston — 344
4. T P B Smith — 330
5. T E Bailey — 320
6. G A Gooch — 289
7. P A Perrin — 284
8. C A G Russell — 280
9. D J Insole — 279
10. M S Nichols — 279

Most Wickets
1. T P B Smith — 1610
2. M S Nichols — 1608
3. T E Bailey — 1593
4. W Mead — 1472
5. J K Lever — 1462
6. J W H T Douglas — 1443
7. R Smith — 1317
8. K C Preston — 1155
9. R E East — 1010
10. L C Eastman — 975

Most Runs
1. K W R Fletcher — 29,374
2. P A Perrin — 29,172
3. J O'Connor — 27,819
4. C A G Russell — 23,610
5. G Barker — 21,895
6. T E Bailey — 21,460
7. G A Gooch — 21,299
8. D J Insole — 20,113
9. C P McGahey — 19,079
10. T C Dodds — 18,565

Most Centuries
1. J O'Connor — 71
2. P A Perrin — 65
3. C A G Russell — 62
4. G A Cooch — 59
5. K S McEwan — 52
6. D J Insole — 48
7. K W R Fletcher — 45
8. G Barker — 30
9. C P McGahey — 29
10. B R Hardie — 27

Most International Appearances
1. G A Gooch — 83
2. T E Bailey — 61
3. K W R Fletcher — 59
4. B R Knight — 29
5. N A Foster — 28
6. J W H T Douglas — 23
7. { K D Boyce — 21
   { J K Lever — 21
9. K Barnes — 15
10. { F L Lane — 14
    { M S Nichols — 14

Batting Averages			*Bowling Averages*		
1.	G A Gooch	48.08	1. {	K Farnes	19.30
2.	K S McEwan	43.37	1. {	W Mead	19.30
3.	C A G Russell	40.91	3.	C J Kortright	20.53
4.	D J Insole	38.67	4.	M D Nichols	21.26
5.	K W R Fletcher	36.99	5.	F G Bull	21.70
6.	P A Perrin	36.19	6.	G M Louden	21.84
7.	J O'Connor	35.21	7.	T E Bailey	21.99
8.	T E Bailey	34.50	8.	B R Knight	22.55
9.	B R Hardie	34.31	9.	J W H T Douglas	23.32
10.	T N Pearce	33.96	10.	N A Foster	23.21

Highest Scores

1.	P A Perrin	343*	v Derbyshire	1904
2.	J R Freeman	286	v Northamptonshire	1921
3.	C P McGahey	277	v Derbyshire	1905
4.	G A Gooch	275	v Kent	1988
5.	C A G Russell	273	v Northamptonshire	1921
6.	J O'Connor	248	v Surrey	1934
7.	J Cutmore	238*	v Gloucestershire	1927
8.	K W R Fletcher	228*	v Sussex	1968
9.	A V Avery	224	v Northamptonshire	1952
10.	D J Insole	219*	v Yorkshire	1949

Also:

P A Perrin	245	v Derbyshire	1912
J O'Connor	237	v Somerset	1933
C P McGahey	230	v Northamptonshire	1908
	225	v Nottinghamshire	1904
G A Gooch	227	v Derbyshire	1984
	220	v Hampshire	1984

Non Cricketing Greats

P Prichard	245	v Leicestershire	1990
L P Crawley	222	v Glamorgan	1928

ESSEX CRICKETING GREATS

Batting Averages up to the end of the 1990 season

	Matches	Innings	NO	Runs	H.Sc	Ave	100s
D L Acfield	378	353	191	1,259	38	7.77	0
A V Avery	268	453	35	14,045	224	33.60	25
T E Bailey	482	774	152	21,460	205	34.50	22
G Barker.............	444	797	46	21,895	181*	29.15	30
M J Bear.............	322	562	44	12,564	137	24.25	9
K D Boyce	211	319	18	6,848	147*	22.75	3
C P Buckenham..	258	394	63	4,882	124	14.74	2
F G Bull.............	88	125	31	1,171	41*	12.45	0
H Carpenter.......	262	466	24	13,043	199	29.50	22
J Cutmore.........	342	593	36	15,937	238*	28.61	15
T C Dodds.........	380	663	17	18,565	157	28.73	17
J W H T Douglas .	459	746	108	17,915	210*	28.07	18
R East	405	513	111	7,103	113	17.66	1
L C Eastman	442	679	49	12,965	161	20.57	7
B E Edmeades	335	555	69	12,593	163	25.91	14
F L Lane............	292	512	30	12,599	217	26.13	18
K Farnes............	79	94	31	590	97*	9.36	0
K W R Fletcher...	572	916	122	29,374	228*	36.99	45
N A Foster.........	140	154	37	2,402	101	20.53	1
J R Freeman	336	577	56	14,507	286	27.84	26
P A Gibb	145	250	12	6,328	141	26.58	8
G A Gooch	295	486	43	21,299	275	48.08	59
W Greensmith	371	550	149	8,042	138*	20.05	1
B R Hardie.........	374	601	78	17,945	162	34.31	27
A B Hipkin	231	326	55	4,239	108	15.64	2
R N S Hobbs......	325	429	102	4,069	100	12.44	2
D J Insole	345	574	54	20,113	219*	38.67	48
B R Knight.........	239	399	42	8,798	165	24.68	8
C J Kortright	160	255	18	4,182	131	17.64	2
J K Lever	439	443	168	2,830	91	10.29	0
G M Louden	82	125	33	844	74	9.17	0
K S McEwan	282	458	41	18,088	218	43.37	52
C P McGahey.....	400	685	61	19,079	277	30.57	29
W Mead	332	469	125	3,843	119	11.17	1
M S Nichols	418	664	66	15,736	205	26.31	20
J O'Connor	516	866	76	27,819	248	35.21	71
H G Owen..........	133	222	17	4,459	134	21.75	3
T N Pearce.........	231	376	48	11,139	211*	33.96	20
P A Perrin	525	894	88	29,172	343*	36.19	65
N Phillip...........	144	201	22	3,784	134	21.13	1
K C Preston	391	460	165	3,024	70	10.25	0
D R Pringle........	171	231	40	4,729	128	24.76	3
W Reeves	271	422	34	6,451	135	16.62	3
C A G Russell	379	628	51	23,610	273	40.91	62
T P B Smith	434	647	115	9,652	163	18.14	8
R Smith.............	419	646	81	11,125	147	19.69	6
B Taylor	539	901	69	18,240	135	21.92	9
S Turner............	354	503	98	9,264	121	22.87	4
F H Vigar	256	397	62	8,660	144	25.58	11
T H Wade..........	e18	472	135	4,972	96	14.75	0
H I Young	128	186	50	1,413	44	10.38	0

ESSEX CRICKETING GREATS

Bowling Averages up to the end of the 1990 season

	Runs	Wkts	Ave	BB	5wl	10wm	Ct/St
D L Acfield	23,509	855	27.49	8-55	30	4	120
A V Avery	627	9	69.66	1-11	0	0	119
T E Bailey	35,042	1,593	21.99	10-90	91	10	320
G Barker	200	5	40.00	2-34	0	0	232
M J Bear	53	0	::::::	::::::	0	0	113
K D Boyce	15,704	662	23.72	9-61	30	6	181
C P Buckenham	24,629	934	26.36	8-33	72	16	143
F G Bull	7,923	365	21.70	9-93	29	5	41
H Carpenter	2,163	46	47.02	4-57	0	0	220
J Cutmore	687	11	62.45	2-31	0	0	121
T C Dodds	1,053	35	30.08	4-34	0	0	176
J W H T Douglas	33,653	1,443	23.32	9-47	93	21	265
R East	25,804	1,010	25.54	8-30	49	10	251
L C Eastman	26,102	975	26.77	7-28	29	3	254
B E Edmeades	9,688	374	25.90	7-37	10	1	105
F L Fane	32	0	::::::	::::::	0	0	141
K Farnes	7,086	367	'19.30	8-38	28	5	42
K W R Fletcher	1,268	29	43.72	5-41	1	0	517
N A Foster	18,529	767	24.16	8-107	42	7	92
J R Freeman	365	10	36.50	3-31	0	0	230/46
P A Gibb	4	0	::::::	::::::	0	0	273/63
G A Gooch	7,370	213	34.46	7-14	3	0	427
W Greensmith	20,711	720	28.76	8-59	21	2	147
B R Hardie	254	3	84.67	2-39	0	0	349
A P Hipkin	13,377	518	25.82	8-71	18	3	209
R N S Hobbs	19,844	763	26.00	8-63	32	5	222
D J Insole	4,061	119	34.12	5-22	1	0	279/1
B R Knight	17,162	761	22.55	8-69	39	8	171
C J Kortright	9,036	440	20.53	8-57	35	8	167
J K Lever	34,348	1,462	23.49	8-37	77	14	157
G M Louden	9,036	415	21.84	8-36	33	5	54
K S McEwan	301	4	75.25	1-0	0	0	197
C P McGahey	9,481	306	30.98	7-27	12	3	140
W Mead	28,423	1,472	19.30	9-40	117	30	151
M S Nichols	34,201	1,608	21.26	9-32	108	22	279
J O'Connor	17,523	537	32.63	7-52	17	2	215/1
H G Owen	321	9	35.66	2-37	0	0	38
T N Pearce	927	15	61.80	4-12	0	0	144
P A Perrin	740	16	46.25	3-13	0	0	284
N Phillip	10,638	423	25.14	6-4	18	1	45
K C Preston	30,288	1,155	26.22	7-55	37	2	344
D R Pringle	16,343	626	26.11	7-18	22	3	127
W Reeves	16,137	581	27.77	7-33	37	5	115
C A G Russell	7,480	276	27.10	5-25	5	0	280
T P B Smith	42,314	1,610	26.28	9-77	117	27	330
R Smith	39,817	1,317	30.23	8-63	73	10	179
B Taylor	21	1	21.00	1-16	0	0	1040/191
S Turner	20,987	810	25.90	6-26	27	1	215
F H Vigar	8,958	236	37.95	8-128	8	0	195
T H Wade	1,391	47	29.59	5-65	1	0	413/177
H I Young	9,092	368	24.70	8-54	18	3	59

Wicket-Keeping

	Matches	Caught	Stmp	Total	Average Number of Victims per match
J.R. Freeman*.......	336	230	46	276	0.82
P.A. Gibb	145	273	63	336	2.31
B. Taylor	539	1,040	191	1,231	2.28
T.H. Wade*..........	318	413	177	590	1.85

* Many matches as a pure batsman/bowler.